Intermediate

D0314209

Just

For class or self-study

Listening and Speaking

Jeremy Harmer

 **Marshall Cavendish**
Education

The *Just* Series

The *Just* series is an integrated series of books that can be used on their own or, when used together, make up a complete course with a consistent methodological approach. The *Just* series is designed for individual skills and language development either as part of a classroom-based course
or a self-study programme. The approach is learner-centred, and each unit has clear aims, motivating topics and interesting practice activities.

   The *Just* series is for adult intermediate learners and can be used as general preparation material for exams at this level.

The *Just* series has four titles:

Just Listening and Speaking 978-0-462-00714-4
Just Reading and Writing 978-0-462-00711-3
Just Grammar 978-0-462-00713-7
Just Vocabulary 978-0-462-00712-0

Photo acknowledgements

p8 Reeve Photography; p10 zefa/Studio Wartenberg; p12 Andi Duff/Alamy; p14 left to right: Mark Sykes/Alamy; Mark Lewis/Alamy; image100/Alamy; Abode/Alamy; p18 Corbis; Pictures Colour Library; Sami Sarkis/Alamy; Mark Andersen/RubberBall/Alamy; Jackson Smith/Alamy; Ken Hawkins/Focus Group, LLC/Alamy; Image Source Ltd/Alamy; John Foxx/Alamy; bottom left to right: Mark Anderson/Alamy; jackson smith/Alamy; Ken Hawkins/Alamy; Image Source/Alamy; John Foxx/Alamy; p44 Mike Egerton/Empics; p46 left to right: Dave Jimenez; Peter Bowater/Alamy; Art Explosion/Recreation; p58 Portrait of John Evelyn (1620-1706) by English School (17th century) Roy Miles Fine Paintings/Bridgeman Art Library; The Artist's Daughter, c. 1927-28 (oil on canvas by Augustus Edwin John (1878-1961) National Gallery of Victoria, Melbourne, Australia/Bridgeman Art Library Felton Bequest; Mr and Mrs Andrews, c. 1748-9 (oil on canvas))(detail of 467) by Thomas Gainsborough (1727-88) National Gallery London UK/Bridgeman Art Library

Text acknowledgements

p59 ©J Dent, 1997, reprinted by permission of Pearson Education Ltd

Audio acknowledgements

p59 ©J Dent, 1997, reproduced by permission of Pearson Education Ltd; So Smooth, Carter Steve (g/Parricell), Bruton Music Ltd (GB2), BRS 23. The Tango Dancer, Shaw Howard/Shaw Howard, Chappell Recorded Music Library, CHAP 133

Marshall Cavendish Education
5th Floor
32–38 Saffron Hill
London
EC1N 8FH

Designed by Hart McLeod Ltd, Cambridge
Printed and bound by Times Offset (M) Sdn Bhd

Contents

Introduction

For the student

Just Listening and Speaking (Intermediate) is part of an integrated series of books designed for you to study on your own, or together with other students and a teacher. It will help you improve your listening and speaking skills in English.

We have chosen the listening extracts and speaking tasks carefully to offer an interesting and challenging mix of topics and activities. With the listening extracts there are exercises to help you understand them and learn new language from them. In the speaking activities we help you do the tasks successfully. You can also listen to other people doing the same tasks.

There is an accompanying CD with all the listening extracts and speaking examples. When you see this symbol ( ) it means that you can listen to the CD. You will also find an audioscript near the back of the book.

When you see this symbol ( ) it means that the answers to the exercises are in the answer key at the back of the book. You can check your answers there.

We are confident that this book will help you become a better listener and speaker of English. Enjoy using it!

For the teacher

The *Just* series is a flexible set of teaching materials that can be used on their own, or in any combination, or as a set to form a complete integrated course. The *Just* series has been written and designed using a consistent methodological approach that allows the books to be used easily together. Each book in the series specialises in either language skills or aspects of the English language. It can be used either in class or by students working on their own.

Just Listening and Speaking is different from the three other books in the *Just* series in that it consists of two parts. In Part A there are 20 listening extracts which include stories, news broadcasts, authentic interviews, radio commercials, discussion and dramatic scenarios. There are comprehension and language extension activities to accompany each listening extract. In Part B there are 10 speaking tasks including taking part in interviews, instructing, reading aloud, story reconstruction and picture memory games. All of these are designed for students either working on their own and interacting with the CD or working in class with a teacher.

All the listening extracts are on the accompanying CD together with example versions of the speaking tasks. There is an audioscript at the back of the book, together with a comprehensive answer key where students can check their work.

We are confident that you will find this book a real asset and that you will also want to try the other books in the series: *Just Reading and Writing*, *Just Vocabulary* and *Just Grammar*.

Part A: Listening

Working in a man's world

1 Listen to Track 1. This is an extract from an interview with 22-year-old April Considine. Can you guess which of the following is her occupation?

- teacher
- design engineer
- doctor
- pilot

Now read the text at the bottom of the next page (9) to see if you were right.

2 Listen to Track 2 and answer the following questions.

a Who first encouraged April to be interested in engineering?

....

b On the whole, does April think that being a woman in a male environment is a good thing or a bad thing?

....

3 Are the following sentences *True* or *False*? Write *T* or *F* in the brackets.

a April's father is Irish.	[ ]
b A glider is an aeroplane without an engine.	[ ]
c April can fly a glider.	[ ]
d April sometimes works at Marshall's at the weekend.	[ ]
e April's work is usually checked by four other people.	[ ]
f A hangar is a big building where you put aeroplanes.	[ ]
g April works in the hangars.	[ ]
h There were many girls in the hangars.	[ ]
i Nobody spoke to April in the hangars.	[ ]

4 Check the meaning of the following phrases. Listen to Track 2 again and tick (✓) the things that April says are important in her job. Put a cross (✗) beside the things that she does not mention.

It is important to:

a	... arrive and leave work on time	[ ]	i	... be good-looking	[ ]
b	... be a hard worker	[ ]	j	... be organised	[ ]
c	... be able to communicate	[ ]	k	... be well-dressed	[ ]
d	... be able to prove yourself	[ ]	l	... be young and enthusiastic	[ ]
e	... be able to work on your own	[ ]	m	... go out in the evening with colleagues	[ ]
f	... be decisive	[ ]	n	... love your job	[ ]
g	... be courteous	[ ]	o	... make sure it's right	[ ]
h	... be energetic	[ ]	p	... show initiative	[ ]

5 April used the following expressions in Track 2. Explain the meaning of the words and phrases in blue.

a He's always been really keen on engineering.

....

b He's always working on cars and bits and pieces.

....

c He did a little bit himself.

....

d I got involved with that.

....

e It still comes down to you.

....

f ... if you sit there and just do the minimum.

....

g They all keep an eye on what I'm doing.

....

h ... to find out how I was getting on.

....

At the age of 22, April Considine has just won the UK 'Young woman of the year' engineering award. After school she went to train with a company called Marshall's Aerospace in Cambridge, UK. She now works there as a design engineer. She is one of only six women in the company, where there are 250 employees.

At Marshall's Aerospace, customers often bring their aeroplanes to be changed in some way. Perhaps they want a new door, or new seats inside the plane. They might want to add something to the wing or have a new video system. It is April's job – along with her colleagues – to design the necessary changes.

On the lawn

1 Look at the picture. A garden can be a dangerous place for a child if there is no adult there. Look at the sentences and write the name of the things in the picture that you think each sentence refers to.

a A child could fall into it.

....

b A child could fall off it.

....

c A child could cut themselves on it.

....

d A child might find something dangerous in it.

....

2 Two people are talking about a dangerous situation in a garden.

a Listen to Track 3 and answer the following questions.

  1 How old was the narrator?..

  2 What had the narrator's mother done? Why?..

  3 'I think I know what's coming.' Can you guess what's going to happen next?..

....

b Listen to Track 4 and answer the following questions.

  1 Why did the narrator get in the trunk?..

....

  2 What happened immediately after that and what did the narrator do?..

  3 'So what happened?' Can you guess?..

c Listen to Track 5 and answer the following questions.

  1 What did the narrator's mother suddenly realise?

....

  2 What did she see? ....

  3 What did she do and how did the narrator feel?..

....

3 What do the following words, used in Tracks 4 and 5, mean?

    a pirate: ....

    b trapped: ....

    c upstairs: ....

    d unconscious: ....

    e shocked: ....

    f claustrophobic: ....

4 Listen to Tracks 3 to 5 again and complete the sentences below with the missing words.

    a ... there was an incident once, well, it could have ended in

       tragedy. It was ....

    b ... and almost immediately got the idea that one of the trunks could be a boat, a pirate ship, that kind of thing. I thought it

       ....

       ....

    c What do you think? Of course I was. Pretty soon

       ....

       .... to be honest.

    d It only took her a second to realise what had happened. She

       ....

    e ... she pulled me out, half-unconscious, ...

       .... and frightened out of my wits!

The parachute jump

1 Listen to the news report on Track 6. Are the following sentences *True* or *False*? Write *T* or *F* in the brackets.

a Someone died. [   ]

b A parachute failed to open properly. [   ]

c The second parachute opened properly. [   ]

d Two people broke bones. [   ]

e The man has terrible injuries, the woman is less seriously injured. [   ]

f It was the woman's first parachute jump. [   ]

g The woman wants to do a parachute jump again. [   ]

2 Listen to Track 6 again and answer the questions with the names from the box.

Beverly
Dennis
Jim
Kevin
Peter
Sue

Who:

a ... parachuted together? ....

b ... is reporting from France? ....

c ... is in the studio in London? ....

d ... is in hospital? ....

e ... reported from the United Nations? ....

f ... was on honeymoon? ....

g ... thinks it was just pure luck? ....

h ... has a broken leg, a broken ankle and two broken feet? ....

i ... has just a broken leg? ....

j ... enjoys seeing the daylight and the birds? ....

3 Complete the audioscript with words and phrases from the box.

emergency chute

faster and faster

first parachute (x2)

going to die

hit the ground

pure luck

second, emergency parachute

solve the problem

REPORTER: The accident happened when the (a) .... didn't open. Mr McIlwee tried to (b) ...., but when he couldn't, he tried to get rid of that chute and use the (c) .... that skydivers always carry with them. A few hours ago I spoke to Beverly's father, Dennis Murtaugh, who explains what happened next. His words are spoken by an actor because the line was not good when we talked.

DENNIS: Unfortunately, Kevin wasn't able to jettison the (d) .... properly so the (e) .... wouldn't open and they just fell (f) .... Kevin told me that they thought that was it, they were (g) ....

REPORTER: So how did they survive?

DENNIS: It was (h) .... I mean they only had half a parachute to slow them down. They (i) .... at an absolutely fantastic speed. It could have killed them.

Listen to Track 6 to check if you were correct.

Commercials

1 Listen to the radio commercials on Track 7. Which is the odd one out (1, 2, 3 or 4)? Why?

....

....

2 Match the commercials (1–4) with these pictures.

a ....   b ....   c ....   d ....

3 Listen to Track 7 again. Answer these questions.

a 500 what? ....

b We're here to help you with what? ....

c 400 what for what? ....

d 350 what for what? ....

e One in three what? ....

f Don't kid who? ....

g Kill what? ....

h Hate what? ....

i Book your holidays from where? ....

4 Which is the best commercial? Why?

....

....

....

5 Complete the following phrases from the radio commercials.

a Help is ....

b Just one of the .... we've got for you.

c .... at any branch …

d Announcing the great Furniture Fanfare ....

e We've got everything .... at prices

   ....

f .... is the click of a mouse.

g The place everyone ....

6 How would you say the following slogans from the end of four radio commercials? Practise saying them as enthusiastically as you can.

a The Galaxy Pronto! The car everyone's talking about!
b Come and see us at the Rialto restaurant. We're here to serve you.
c For a great day out visit the Russia Park. You won't regret it.
d Don't delay! Buy your new computer today.

7 You are going to write a radio commercial for a product.

a Choose one of the following products or think of your own:
   • car
   • chocolate bar
   • mobile phone
   • pair of trainers
   • computer game
   • fizzy/soft drink.

b Complete the following chart.

What is the product?	
What are its main selling points (price, what's special about it, convenience, etc.)?	
Describe the characters and situation for the commercial (e.g. two men in a lift, two women in a café).	
What is the 'punchline' (e.g. '*We're here to help you with all those numbers*')?	
What music and/or sound effects will you use in the commercial?	

c Now write your commercial. You can use language from Exercise 5 or from the audioscript for Track 7, on page 66. Record your commercial onto a tape. Does it sound good?

The questionnaire

1 Listen to the interview on Track 8. As you listen to the man's answers, cross out any information that is incorrect in the questionnaire below, and write in the correct answer. The first one is done for you.

QUESTIONNAIRE FORM 03657

(For each question, tick the appropriate box.)

Q1 How often do you go shopping?

once a week	[✓]
twice a week	[✓]
three times a week	[ ]
more than three times	[ ]

Q2 How many items do you buy when you go shopping?

1 item	[✓]
2 items	[ ]
3–5 items	[ ]
6–10 items	[ ]
10+ items	[ ]

Q3 How much time do you spend when you go shopping?

0–59 minutes	[✓]
1–2 hours	[ ]
more than 2 hours	[ ]

Q4 What do you buy most often?

trousers	[ ]
shirts	[✓]
underwear	[ ]
T-shirts	[ ]
jackets	[ ]
sweaters	[ ]

Q5 Favourite colour (state item of clothing)?

....

....

....

**GRAND HOLIDAY
PRIZE DRAW**

**HOLIDAY FOR TWO
IN JAMAICA**

2 Rearrange the words in brackets to make sentences from the interview. Then listen to Track 8 again. Which reply (from the box below) follows each sentence? The first one is done for you.

> 1 Oh yes I do. I never win anything!
> 2 Look this is really ...
> 3 OK, the fourth question ...
> 4 Right, well the first question is ....
> 5 Sorry?
> 6 The same as anybody else's, I suppose.
> 7 It'll only take a second.
> 8 Yes ... and how many items do you usually buy ... ?

a (a/a/bit/hurry/of/I'm/./in)

I'm in a bit of a hurry. .... [7]

b (automatically/be/draw/entered/in our prize/./You'll)

.... [ ]

c (are/chances/of/?/my/What/winning)

.... [ ]

d (I/know/./wouldn't)

.... [ ]

e (a/get/let's/move on/./But)

.... [ ]

f (have/I/if/./only/to/But)

.... [ ]

g (do/for fun/I/It's/not/./something)

.... [ ]

h (be/./Don't/know/never/./You/pessimistic/so)

.... [ ]

Types of holiday

1 Look at the holidays. In your opinion, which one is:

a ... the most expensive? ....

b ... the most comfortable? ....

c ... the most energetic? ....

d ... the most enjoyable? ....

e ... the one you really do not want to try? ....

2 Before you listen to Track 9, look at the five people in these pictures. Who likes which type of holiday, shown in Exercise 1, do you think? Make notes of your answers below.

Tony

Sandra

Josette

Meera

Steve

a a package holiday ....

b a sightseeing holiday ....

c a backpacking holiday ....

d a cruise ....

e a camping holiday ....

Now listen to Track 9. Were you correct?

3 Listen to Track 9 again.

Who:

a ... doesn't like tourist resorts? ....

b ... has tried water-skiing? ....

c ... loves a bit of luxury? ....

d ... has children who go swimming and boating? ....

e ... doesn't sunbathe? ....

f ... has been to Scotland? ....

g ... likes nightlife and clubbing? ....

h ... likes places off the beaten track? ....

i ... likes galleries and museums? ....

4 Use the following diagram as a start for your own holiday wordmap. Use words from Exercises 1–3. You can also look at the audioscript of Track 9 on page 67 to find more holiday words. How many more words can you add to the wordmap?

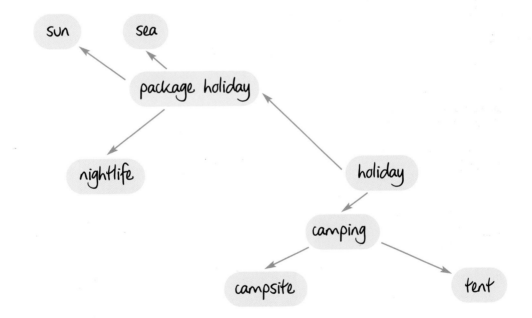

●●● ## Travel announcements

1 When you are travelling, when and where do you hear public announcements? What do they usually say?

. . . .

2 When would you hear these announcements? Look at the pictures (a–g) and listen to the announcements on Track 10. Write the number of the announcement (1–7) above the appropriate picture.

a ....

b ....

M	TIME	DESTINATI
2	6:40	BIRMINGHA
1	6:52	KING'S LYN
3	6:55	MANCHESTE
1	6:59	LIVERPOOL
4	7:00	LONDON KIN

c ....

d ....

FG0902	GATE CLOSED
BA2409	NOW BOARDING
BA2018	WAIT IN LOUNGE
VA0034	WAIT IN LOUNGE
TV0102	WAIT IN LOUNGE
BA0208	DELAYED
KL0123	WAIT IN LOUNGE
DA134	WAIT IN LOUNGE

e ....

MANCHESTER AIR

f ....

GATE 24

g ....

3   Complete these expressions from the announcements with the words or phrases from the box. Match them with the pictures (the first one is done for you).

announcement	position
board	proceed
delay	regret
fasten	return
fastened	running
last call	shouldn't
late	sorry
place	switched off

a This is the _last call_ for flight 2409.   [d]

b Please .... to gate number 35.   [ ]

c Here is a platform ....   [ ]

d We are ready to .... the aircraft.   [ ]

e We .... to announce the .... of the 12.35.   [ ]

f The train is .... approximately 15 minutes ....   [ ]

g .... for the delay.   [ ]

h We .... be here for too long.   [ ]

i Will all passengers please .... to your seats.   [ ]

j .... your seatbelts.   [ ]

k .... your seats in the upright ....   [ ]

l Please keep your seatbelts .... until the captain has .... the seatbelt sign.   [ ]

Listen to Track 10 again to check your answers.

'Making myself homeless' (a song)

1 Think about your home. Write five adjectives to describe:

a ... what it looks like.

b ... what it feels like.

2 Match the phrases on the left with their meanings on the right.

a a sense of freedom — someone who thinks everything will be terrible

b a camper van → a feeling that you are free

c to hit the road — a van that you can sleep in

d Home is where the heart is. — to feel as if you do not have any friends

e to be homeless — to not have a home

f to be lonely — someone who thinks everything will be wonderful

g an optimist — anywhere that you feel comfortable is home

h a pessimist — to go travelling

3 You are going to hear a song called 'Making myself homeless'. Here are the first and last verses. What order should the lines go in? Write the numbers in the brackets.

First verse:

a [   ] I don't feel like staying in

b [   ] I'm sitting here without you

c [   ] It's cold and it's empty

d [   ] The light is getting dim

Last verse:

e [   ] And my travelling days will be done

f [   ] And we'll have our new day in the sun

g [   ] And we'll go back home one fine morning

h [   ] And you'll come running towards me

Listen to the song on Track 11. Did you get the first and the last verses right?

4 Which of these summaries (a–c) best describes the song?

   a The singer is unhappy because his camper van is cold and empty, and it is raining. He wants to travel to the road's end.

   b The singer is unhappy because his girlfriend has left him. He leaves home and travels in a camper van. He hopes he will meet his girlfriend again and that they will go back home together.

   c The singer is unhappy because his house is cold and empty so he decides to go on the road. It rains a lot, but he's looking forward to a day when it will be sunny again.

5 Complete these lines from the song.

   a I guess I'll ....

   b I'm not a .... or an ....

   c I just need to have ....

   d And the light is .... at the road's

      ....

   e I'll forget about you if ....

   f And the road stretches ....

   g I can do whatever ....

   h What use is travelling .... ?

   i Just makes me homesick for ....

   j The road leads on ....

6 Listen to Track 11 again and follow the lyrics in the audioscript on page 67.

   Complete this sentence:

   I like/don't like the song because: ....

   ....

   ....

   ....

Looking round a house

1 Listen to Track 12 and number the pictures in the order in which they are talked about.

bathroom

a ....

living room

b ....

second bedroom

c ....

main bedroom

d ....

kitchen

e ....

2 **Which room:**

a ... doesn't have space for much furniture?

....

b ... is nice to look out of (and isn't a bedroom)?

....

c ... can always be made warm?

....

d ... do they both like a lot?

....

e ... has some interesting furniture?

....

f ... could be either for sleeping or working?

....

g ... doesn't get any light from outside?

....

3 **Answer these questions.**

a How long has the house been empty?

....

b Why did the last tenants leave the house?

....

c What is Paul doing at the moment?

....

d What does Hilary do normally?

....

e What is she doing at the moment?

....

f What is the final decision about the house, and who makes it?

....

(To find out how Paul and Hilary got on in their new house, look at LISTENING 11, 'Haunted house'.)

Haunted house

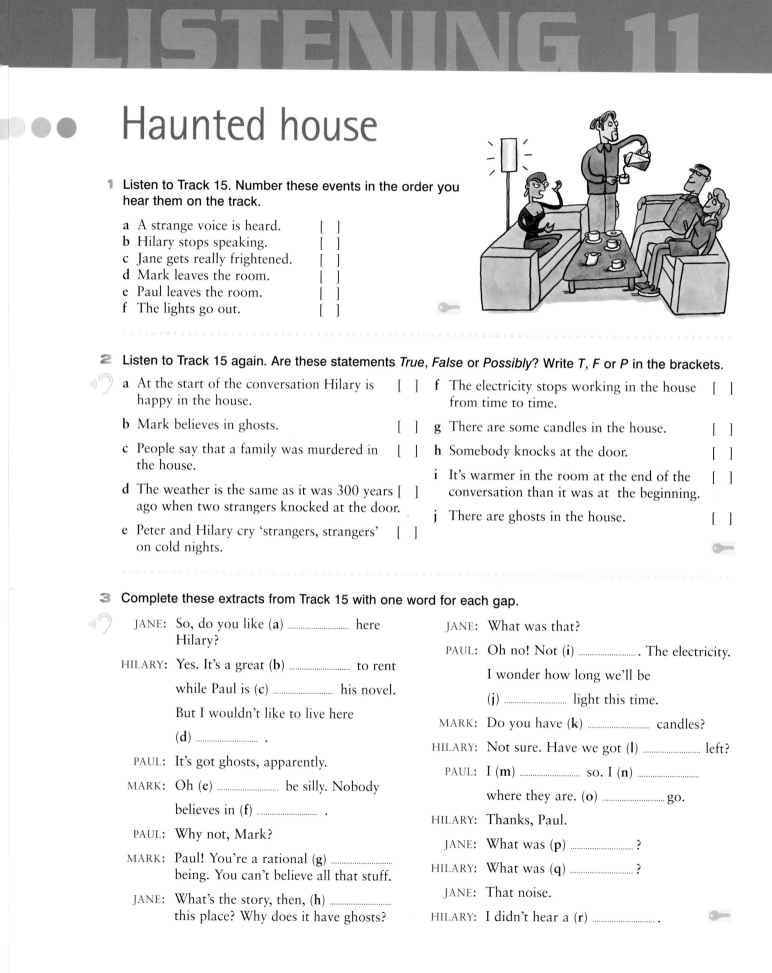

1 Listen to Track 15. Number these events in the order you hear them on the track.

a A strange voice is heard.　　　　[　]
b Hilary stops speaking.　　　　　[　]
c Jane gets really frightened.　　　[　]
d Mark leaves the room.　　　　　[　]
e Paul leaves the room.　　　　　[　]
f The lights go out.　　　　　　　[　]

2 Listen to Track 15 again. Are these statements *True*, *False* or *Possibly*? Write *T*, *F* or *P* in the brackets.

a At the start of the conversation Hilary is happy in the house.　[　]

b Mark believes in ghosts.　[　]

c People say that a family was murdered in the house.　[　]

d The weather is the same as it was 300 years ago when two strangers knocked at the door.　[　]

e Peter and Hilary cry 'strangers, strangers' on cold nights.　[　]

f The electricity stops working in the house from time to time.　[　]

g There are some candles in the house.　[　]

h Somebody knocks at the door.　[　]

i It's warmer in the room at the end of the conversation than it was at the beginning.　[　]

j There are ghosts in the house.　[　]

3 Complete these extracts from Track 15 with one word for each gap.

JANE: So, do you like (a) .... here Hilary?

HILARY: Yes. It's a great (b) .... to rent while Paul is (c) .... his novel. But I wouldn't like to live here (d) ....

PAUL: It's got ghosts, apparently.

MARK: Oh (e) .... be silly. Nobody believes in (f) ....

PAUL: Why not, Mark?

MARK: Paul! You're a rational (g) .... being. You can't believe all that stuff.

JANE: What's the story, then, (h) .... this place? Why does it have ghosts?

JANE: What was that?

PAUL: Oh no! Not (i) .... The electricity. I wonder how long we'll be (j) .... light this time.

MARK: Do you have (k) .... candles?

HILARY: Not sure. Have we got (l) .... left?

PAUL: I (m) .... so. I (n) .... where they are. (o) .... go.

HILARY: Thanks, Paul.

JANE: What was (p) .... ?

HILARY: What was (q) .... ?

JANE: That noise.

HILARY: I didn't hear a (r) ....

anyone	paul
around	paul
cold	paul
cold	playing
else	strangers
hear	strangers
house	suddenly
house	that
in	the
in	the
it's	you

4 Without looking at the audioscript (or listening to Track 15 again) can you use the words in the box to reassemble 5 lines of the dialogue? Use each word once only. Pay attention to capital letters, full stops (.), question marks (?) and exclamation marks (!).

JANE: I'm really cold. (a). ....

....

HILARY: (b) Yes. *Suddenly* ....

....

GHOSTLY VOICE; (c) ....

....

JANE: (d) Did ....

....

MARK: (e) *It's just* ....

....

Check your answers by listening to Track 15 and reading the audioscript on page 69.

Weather forecast

1 Complete the following diagram.

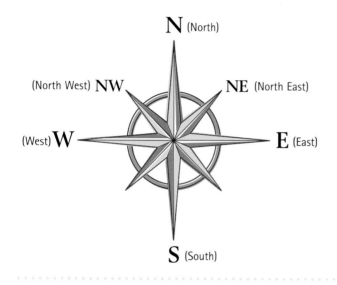

N (North)

(North West) NW   NE (North East)

(West) W ——————— E (East)

S (South)

2 Match the terms on the left with the symbols on the right.

a cloudy with sunny periods [   ]

b cloudy, light rain [   ]

c raining heavily [   ]

d heavy cloud [   ]

e snow [   ]

f heavy snow [   ]

g two degrees centigrade [   ]

1

2

3

4

5

6

7

3 Listen to Track 16 and answer the questions.

a What time of day is it? ....

b What is the warmest part of the country in the afternoon? ....

c What is the coldest part of the country in the afternoon? ....

d Where is Samantha going this afternoon?

....

4 Listen to Track 16 again, as many times as you want, and draw the symbols (in the box) on the maps. Include the temperature too (e.g. -1°C).

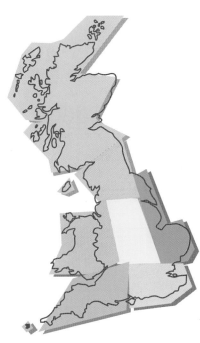

a Now

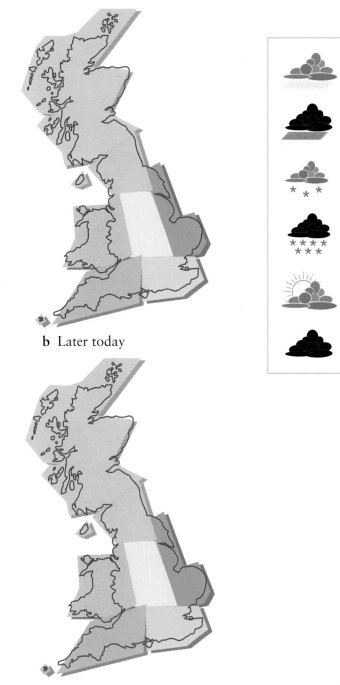

b Later today

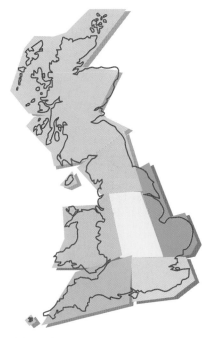

c Tonight

d Tomorrow

The tango

1 Look at the following pictures. What do you think is happening in each one? Write notes.

a

b

c

d

Put the pictures in the correct order to tell the story.

1 ....   2 ....   3 ....   4 ....

2 Listen to the story on Track 17. Were you right?

3 What do you understand by the following American English words and phrases from Track 17?

a sidewalk: ....

b permit: ....

c plates: ....

d precinct: ....

e ma'am: ....

. . . .

4 Listen to Track 17 again. Complete the gaps in these sentences from the track. Use one word for each gap.

a You .... here.   [   ]

b Are you telling us we .... for people?   [   ]

c We .... do.   [   ]

d Well I'm sorry, ma'am, 'might' isn't ....

....   [   ]

e You .... a permit to do this kind of thing.   [   ]

f It's parked illegally so you'd better ....

.... about it.   [   ]

g Do you know .... the tango, officer?   [   ]

h Come on! You .... it.   [   ]

Who says which line? The police officer (PO), the male dancer (MD) or the female dancer (FD)? Write your answer in the brackets after each sentence.

Irritation

1 Look at the pictures (a–d). Listen to Track 18. Number the pictures 1– 4 in the order you hear the scenes.

a [......]

b [......]

c [......]

d [......]

2 Complete the phrases from the conversations. Write which scene above (a–d) the phrases come from. The first one is done for you.

Picture

a Can't you read ...*the sign*............ ?   [*b*]

b Could you turn .... ?   [ ]

c Have you just .... ?   [ ]

d I can't .... I .... can't.   [ ]

e It means you can't ....   [ ]

f It means you .... I suppose.   [ ]

g It's driving ....   [ ]

h What .... mean?   [ ]

i Will you please ....   [ ]

3 Answer the following questions with phrases such as 'the man in picture a', 'the girl in picture d', etc.

Who:

a ... stopped suddenly and dramatically?

....

b ... was upset by a voice?

....

c ... was upset by a sound?

....

d ... was embarrassed by a relation?

....

e ... was sarcastic?

....

f ... had to stop talking to someone?

....

g ... had to pick something up?

....

h ... had to move?

....

The line-up

1 Look at the picture. Why are the men there? Make a note of your answer to this question.

....

....

....

2 Listen to Track 19. Which man (1–7) does the woman choose? ....

3 Listen to Track 19 again. Answer the questions.

a How did the woman get to the police station?

....

b What did someone take from her?

....

c What does the woman say about her eyes?

....

d Why is she unsure about the identity of the thief? ....

4 Without looking at the audioscript (or listening to Track 19 again) can you use the words to reassemble 5 lines of dialogue. Use each word once only. Pay attention to capital letters, full stops (.), question marks (?) and commas (,).

any	me	trouble
brought	me	very
didn't	morning	want
do	much	what
do	my	you
getting	oh	you
good	son	you
have	thank	
here	to	

POLICEMAN: Good morning, Madam.

WOMAN: (a) ....

POLICEMAN: (b) I hope ....

....

WOMAN: (c) No. ....

....

POLICEMAN: (d) ....

WOMAN: (e) So, ...

....

Check your answers by listening to Track 19.

5 Which word fits in all of the gaps in the following extract?

POLICEMAN: Well, who is it?

WOMAN: That ....

POLICEMAN: Which ....?

WOMAN: The .... with the beard.

POLICEMAN: There are three men with beards.

WOMAN: Yes.

POLICEMAN: So which .... is it? Please.

WOMAN: The tall man in a green jacket.

POLICEMAN: Yes, but there are two men with green ...

WOMAN: Look! That ....

POLICEMAN: Which ....?

WOMAN: The .... scratching his ear.

Check your answer with Track 19.

6 Cover the picture. Now write a description of man number 3. When you have finished, look at the picture again. Were you a good witness?

....

....

....

....

....

....

●●● ## Here is the news

1 Listen to Track 20. Which of the following topics are discussed in the news broadcast? Tick (✓) those that are mentioned.

a company collapse   [ ]   [ ]
b computer virus   [ ]   [ ]
c cure for cancer discovered [ ]   [ ]
d earthquake   [ ]   [ ]
e election results   [ ]   [ ]
f Internet romance   [ ]   [ ]
g mountain rescue   [ ]   [ ]
h peace talks   [ ]   [ ]
i plane crash   [ ]   [ ]
j rocket launch for Pluto expedition [ ]   [ ]

In the second column above, number the stories that you have ticked in the order you hear them.

2 Listen to Track 20 again, and then write answers to the questions.

What is the connection between:

a ... a mobile phone and a mountain?

....

b ... K2 and Paris?

....

c ... a computer virus and Puerto Rico?

....

d ... Bella Karsfeld and 'Money for jam'?

....

e ... Oxford and Tuscaloosa?

....

f ... 35 and 65?

....

g ... $70 million and holiday homes?

....

3   Answer the following questions about the news reports.

a   Who was saved from almost certain death?

....

b   Where were there appalling weather conditions?

....

c   Who got over his surprise?

....

d   Who is trying to trace the source of what?

....

e   Who eventually agreed to marry?

....

f   Who had lied about her age?

....

g   Who or what is to cease business?

....

h   Who expects more business failures?

....

4   Look at the audioscript for Track 20 and choose one of the stories. Record it yourself onto a tape. Compare your tape with the original.

Scientists and film makers

1 Listen to the conversation on Track 21. Tick (✓) the words you hear.

a aeroplanes [ ]
b antibiotics [ ]
c aspirin [ ]
d biology [ ]
e cars [ ]
f chemistry [ ]
g computer [ ]
h cry [ ]
i injection [ ]
j laugh [ ]
k medicine [ ]
l physics [ ]
m ships [ ]
n shout [ ]
o space station [ ]
p university [ ]
q whisper [ ]

2 Listen to the Track 21 again. Complete the sentences with 'Tom' or 'Michelle'. The first one is done for you.

a ....Tom.......... speaks first.

b ....'s going to study science at university.

c .... does not approve of film studies as a university course.

d .... is going to do more than one subject at university.

e .... is very surprised by what .... says.

We know this because .... is asked to repeat a statement.

f .... thinks ....'s question is stupid.

g .... uses medicine as a subject to persuade

.... of her point of view.

h .... is worried that some medicines don't work any longer.

i .... thinks that science is the cause of many problems.

j .... uses the common cold to attack

........................'s point of view.

k ....'s going to do a film studies course.

3 What are Tom's criticisms of the things Michelle talks about?
Complete the table.

a	Cars and aeroplanes	1 ....
		2 ....
		3 ....
b	Computers	1 ....
		2 ....
c	Drugs/modern medicines	1 ....
		2 ....

4 Complete this extract from the conversation on Track 21 with one
word in each gap.

MICHELLE: What about medicine?

TOM: What about (a) .... ?

MICHELLE: Well, without science and (b) .... most children
wouldn't survive for more than (c) .... five years,
and if we did (d) .... it into adulthood we'd all be
dead before we were (e) ....

TOM: Well, I ...

MICHELLE: Just think of all the (f) .... that keep people
alive, all of them (g) .... by scientists. Think of
the aspirin you take for a (h) .... , the antibiotics
that cure (i) .... , all of those things.

TOM: Well, if science is so (j) .... , how come we still
don't know how to cure the (k) .... (l) .... ?

MICHELLE: Look, just because ...

TOM: And as for (m) .... , people have taken so many
(n) .... that they don't (o) .... anymore.
There are new (p) .... that are drug-resistant.

MICHELLE: Well yes, but who will (q) .... out how to get
round that (r) .... ?

TOM: I haven't the (s) .... idea.

MICHELLE: (t) .... , of course.

Check your answers by listening to Track 21 again.

● ● ● Reactions

1 What are the people talking about? Listen to Track 22 and match the pictures (a–e) with the conversations (1–5).

a Conversation ....

b Conversation ....

c Conversation ....

d Conversation ....

e Conversation ....

2 Listen to Track 22 again. Write which conversations (1–5) the following sentences refer to.

a One person laughed a lot, the other did not.   Conversation ....**4**....

b One person really wants to talk about the event. The other is not so keen.   Conversation ....
    Conversation ....

c One person thought something was frightening. The other person thought it was quite (but not very) frightening.   Conversation ....

d One person thought something was funny but the other is not so sure.   Conversation ....

e Someone doesn't much like art.   Conversation ....

f The speakers want to see something again.   Conversation ....

g The woman and the man disagree about the picture.   Conversation ....

h Two people agree that a picture is lovely.   Conversation ....

i Two people really enjoyed being scared.   Conversation ....

3 Complete these extracts from Track 22 with one or more words for each gap.

a Look at that girl .... – the way the sunlight .... her hair.

b It's just so full ....

c She doesn't look like .... at all. And all those people ...., they're supposed to be musicians, are they?

d Well, perhaps I just ....

e I could .... most of the time.

f I .... laughing.

g But it was ...., wasn't it?

h There's .... a good piece of live theatre.

Watching the match

1 **Listen to Track 23 and answer the following questions.**

a Who is in the sitting room – Geoff or Angela?...

b Who is in the kitchen – Geoff or Angela? ....

c Who answers the phone the first time? ....

d Who answers the phone the second time? ....

e Who is the first caller? ....

f Who is the second caller? ....

g What is Angela's problem?...

h What does Geoff miss? ....

2 **Listen to Track 23 again. Are the following statements *True* or *False* ? Write *T* or *F* in the brackets.**

a The match is a competition final. [ ]

b The game goes into extra time. [ ]

c The final score is Liverpool 2, Arsenal 3. [ ]

d Geoff's mother has bought a new car. [ ]

e Geoff's mother is sympathetic when Geoff says he wants to watch the football, not talk on the telephone. [ ]

f Geoff's brother can't persuade a girl to go out with him. [ ]

g Geoff's brother is sympathetic when Geoff says he wants to watch the football, not talk on the telephone. [ ]

h A player called Owen scores the winning goal. [ ]

i Angela loves football. [ ]

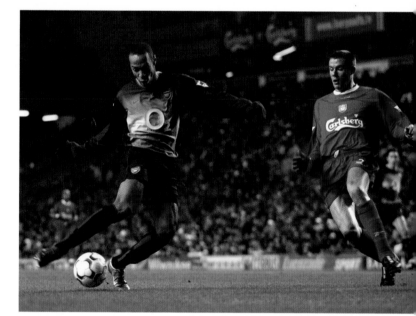

3 In these phone conversations, write what you think the other person is saying based on the words that we hear in Track 23. The first one is done for you.

Conversation 1

GEOFF: Hello? Oh hello (name of caller).

a CALLER: *What are you doing?*

GEOFF: Watching the football. Arsenal against Liverpool

b CALLER: ....?

GEOFF: What?

c CALLER: ....?

GEOFF: Yes, it's nearly finished.

d CALLER: ....

GEOFF: Have you? You've seen a new car you want to buy?

e CALLER: ....

GEOFF: Well, I'm sure you can get a different colour if you don't like red. Look Mum, can I ring you back?

f CALLER: ....?

GEOFF: Yes, of course I want to speak to you.

g CALLER: ....

GEOFF: No, no please don't be upset. I just want to watch the end of this game. You know how important it is.

h CALLER: ....?

GEOFF: Yes, I promise. In about five minutes or so.

Conversation 2

GEOFF: Hello.

a CALLER: ....

GEOFF: Hello (name of caller).

b CALLER: ....

GEOFF: You're feeling unhappy, are you?

c CALLER: ....

GEOFF: Well, if she doesn't want to go out with you I would stop ringing her. But look, can I ring you back? It's the Cup Final.

d CALLER: ....

GEOFF: I know you're my brother.

e CALLER: ....?

GEOFF: Yes, yes, I do care about you. But I'll ring you back.

f CALLER: ....?

GEOFF: Because I don't want to talk right now. Goodbye.

Which Susan?

1 What would you expect to have to do if you had to do the following tests? Write notes.

a an audition for a music group or an orchestra: ....

....

b an audition for a play: ....

....

c an interview for a new job: ....

....

d a trial for a place on a sports team: ....

....

e a language oral exam: ....

....

2 Read the information about the following people. Listen to Track 24 and say which one of the three people you think is talking.

Susan Bakewell is a hospital nurse who works with children. In her spare time she plays the double bass. She has to audition to get into a local orchestra.

Susan Blewitt is an immigration officer. When she is not working, Susan paints pictures of the countryside, and studies Russian. She has a Russian oral exam coming up.

Susan Shellworth is a lawyer, but away from work she spends all her time training at her local athletics track. She's hoping to compete in the next Olympic Games.

3 Listen to Track 25 and answer these questions.

 a Which of the five tests from Exercise 1 was the speaker involved

  in? ....

 b Was she successful or not?

  ....

 c What did the speaker think of the experience?

  ....

4 Match the words and phrases from Track 25 with their definitions.

 a accompanist   a quick rehearsal of a piece of music
 b in tune   a series of notes going up and down with fixed intervals between them
 c run-through   playing the music straight away, the first time you see it
 d scale   usually a pianist who plays along with the solo player
 e sight-reading   when the notes sound right, rather than ugly, because they are not
                         too high or too low

5 Listen to Track 25 again and answer the questions.

 a What three things did the speaker have to do in   **d** What day was the next orchestra practice?
   the audition?
                                                              ....
   ....
                                                            e Who did the speaker phone to talk about the
 b How many people were in the room?   audition?

   ....

 c What day was the audition?   **f** When did the speaker know if she had been
                                                               successful?
   ....
                                                              ....

6 Find the following phrases
   (in blue) in the audioscript for
   Track 25 and match them to
   the meanings (a–f).

What on earth (am I doing here)?	I may as well (go home).
I may as well (see it through.)	I can be out of here.
(I sort of breathed) a huge sigh of relief.	Do I take that as (a 'yes')?

 a a large exhalation of breath because something is finished:

  ....

 b continue until the end: ....

 c I can leave: ....

 d It would be a good idea to: ....

 e Do I understand that to be: ....

 f what (made stronger): ....

Interview role-play

1 Look at the picture of ten different occupations with the accompanying key and complete the following tasks.

a footballer	f soldier
b nurse	g personal assistant (PA)
c designer	h refuse collector
d primary teacher	i journalist
e orchestral conductor	j firefighter

a Which of the ten occupations would you most like to do? (Which is your 'number 1' occupation?) Write the name below.

b Write notes about your 'number 1' occupation. Say what people do in the occupation and why you would like it.

c Which of the ten occupations would you least like to do? (Which is your 'number 10' occupation?) Write the name below.

d Write notes about your 'number 10' occupation. Say what people do in the occupation and why you would not like it.

Example:

a 'Number 1' occupation: ...nurse...

b They look after people.
  They work with people.
  They help people.
  I would like to be a nurse because I could talk to a lot of people
  I would like to be a nurse because I am interested in medicine

Your answer:

a 'Number 1' occupation: ....

b ....

....

....

c 'Number 10' occupation: ....

d ....

....

....

....

2 Chose one of the occupations in Exercise 1. Imagine that it is your occupation. Listen to Track 26 and answer the interviewers' questions.

Example:

INTERVIEWER: Hi. What's your name?
YOU: Staislaw.
INTERVIEWER: What do you do?
YOU: I'm a nurse.
INTERVIEWER: Oh really? Do you like the job?
... etc.

Telling stories

1 Look at the pictures and write answers to the following questions.

Picture A

a How many people are doing the washing up? ....

b Do they (the ones doing the washing up) normally work at the restaurant? ....

c Who else can you see in the picture? ....

....

d How do the people (who are not doing the washing up) feel, do you think? ....

Picture B

e What is the waiter waiting for? ....

....

f How does Pete (the man sitting down) feel? ....

....

g What is he remembering? ....

....

Picture C

h Where are Pete and Tabitha? ....

....

i How are they feeling? ....

....

Picture D

j Where is Pete? ....

k Why has he gone there? ....

l What can he see inside the house? ....

Picture E

m Who are Pete and Tabitha talking to? ....

....

n What is Pete trying to explain? ....

....

o What does the other man think about Pete's explanation? ....

....

p What is he telling Pete and Tabitha to do? ....

....

A

B

C

D

E

2 What is the story of Pete and Tabitha's evening? Use your answers to Exercise 1 to help you put the pictures (A–E) in the correct order (1–5) to tell the story.

1 .... 2 .... 3 .... 4 .... 5 ....

Check your answer in the key.

. . . .

3 Tell the story in Exercise 1 in your own words using your answers in Exercise 1. Use a tape recorder to record what you say.

Listen to what you have recorded and make a note of any corrections you want to make.

Record your story again.

. . . .

4 Now listen to Track 27. The woman is telling the same story about Pete and Tabitha. How similar is her story to yours?

. . . .

5 Write two questions that you would like to ask Pete and Tabitha, and two questions that you would like to ask the manager.

Questions for Pete and Tabitha:

a ....

b ....

Questions for the manager:

c ....

d ....

Now give Pete and Tabitha advice for the future so that they don't have to wash dishes again!

e ....

Drawing homes

1 Look at the picture and put the correct letters in the brackets.

chimney [ ]   fence [ ]   garage [ ]   gate [ ]   window [ ]

2 Listen to Track 29. Draw the picture that is described to you.

3 What instructions would you give to help someone draw the following picture (if they couldn't see it)? Record your instructions onto a tape.

4 Now listen to Track 30. Martha is giving instructions for someone to draw the picture in Exercise 3. Are her instructions the same as yours?

Interviewing a portrait

1 Choose one of the pictures and complete these tasks, using your imagination.

   a Which person have you chosen from pictures 1–3 below? Make notes about their character. Are they kind/unkind, happy/unhappy, etc.?

   ....

   ....

   b What kind of a life do the people lead? Make notes about a typical day in their life.

   ....

   ....

   c What makes them happiest or unhappiest, do you think? Make notes about their likes and hobbies.

   ....

   ....

John Evelyn

Rachel

Mr and Mrs Andrews

2 Now listen to Track 31 and answer the interviewer's questions as if you were one of the people in Exercise 1: John, Rachel, or Mr or Mrs Andrews.

Example:

INTERVIEWER: Hello, what's your name?

YOU: I'm Mrs Andrews.

INTERVIEWER: Oh, nice to meet you. How are you?

YOU: Fine, thanks.

Marianne's dream

1 Read 'Marianne's dream' and answer the questions.

a Who paints pictures? ....

b Who buys the pictures in the dream?

....

c Who buys new clothes and shoes in the dream?

....

d Who goes out for dinner? ....

....

e Who goes round the world? ....

....

f Who becomes famous? ....

....

g When does Marianne have her dream?

....

Marianne's dream

When Marianne started a new picture she often had the same dream when she went to sleep. In the dream she went to Malapa, the biggest city on the mainland. She walked along the main street with her pictures under her arm. She went into a shop and sold them for a lot of money. Then, in her dream, she went to a department store and bought a wonderful dress, some pretty shoes and a beautiful coat.

After that, she went back to the first shop and looked at her pictures in the window. A lot of people were buying them. One man bought three. He was tall, he had dark hair and he was very good-looking.

'Who painted these pictures?' he asked the shop assistant.

'That girl there', came the answer.

The good-looking man walked up to Marianne. 'I've never seen paintings like these before,' he said.

'One day you'll be very famous. People will buy your pictures all over the world.'

Marianne was very happy. 'How do you know that?' she asked.

'Pictures are my business,' he answered. 'I buy and sell them. Will you come and have dinner with me? I want to talk about your paintings.'

They had dinner together. The man said, 'Your paintings are beautiful. But you are even lovelier than your paintings.'

They danced together that night and they fell in love. Soon they were married, and then they went round the world together. Marianne painted hundreds of pictures. She was famous.

That was Marianne's dream.

Adapted from 'David & Marianne' by John Dent.

2 Read 'Marianne's dream' aloud. Underline any words or phrases that are difficult to pronounce.

3 Listen to the reading of 'Marianne's dream' on Track 32. Pay attention to the pronunciation of the words you underlined.

4 Play Track 32 again. This time read aloud along with the speaker on the track.

5 Read the story into a tape recorder. Listen to your recording and compare your voice with the voice on the CD. If you sound very different, read the story again so that you sound more like the voice on the tape.

What can you remember?

1   Look at the picture. Give yourself exactly 50 seconds. Try to remember everything in it.

Now cover the picture.

2   Listen to Track 33. Answer the questions about the picture if you can.

3   Listen to Track 33 again, but this time look at the picture. Answer the questions again. Are your answers different?

4   Listen to someone answering the questions on Track 34.

What are they saying?

1 Look at the pictures and listen to Track 35. The people's voices aren't very clear. Write what you think they are saying.

a

ANNE: ....

JOHN: ....

ANNE: ....

JOHN: ....

ANNE: ....

JOHN: ....

ANNE: ....

JOHN: ....

b

MARIA: ....

CHARLES: ....

MARIA: ....

CHARLES: ....

MARIA: ....

CHARLES: ....

MARIA: ....

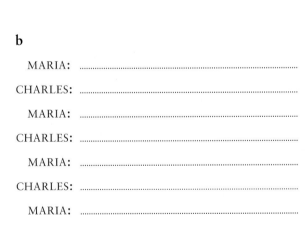

2 Listen to Track 36. This time you will hear the conversations clearly. Were your answers right in Exercise 1?

3 Practise saying the conversations using the same stress and intonation as the speakers on the CD.

4 Play Track 36 again. Say the conversations along with the speakers on the CD. You can take one part in each conversation.

The invitation

1 Look at the picture. Read the conversation below and answer the questions that follow.

AL: Hello.
BOB: Hi. Nice to see you.
AL: Are you well?
BOB: Yes, I'm fine. And you?
AL: Yes, I'm fine too, thanks. Hey, I've got two tickets for the match tonight. D'you want to come?
BOB: Tonight? You've got tickets for the match tonight?
AL: That's what I said.
BOB: And you're offering one of them to me?
AL: Yes, that's the general idea.
BOB: I don't know what to say.
AL: Well, yes or no would be a possibility!
BOB: All right, then, yes please.
AL: Fantastic. Shall I come round to your place or will you come to mine?
BOB: I'll come round to yours if that's OK.
AL: Yes, that's fine. Can you be there by about 6.30?
BOB: That early?
AL: Yes. If we're to get to the match on time.
BOB: OK then. Do you think it's going to be cold?
AL: Dunno. I haven't heard the forecast. But I'd dress up warm if I was you.
BOB: That sounds like pretty good advice.
AL: Look, I've got to go. My lunch hour finished five minutes ago.
BOB: Oh right.
AL: So see you at 6.30?
BOB: Yes, I'll be there. Oh, and thanks a lot.
AL: Don't mention it. Bye.
BOB: Bye.

a What does Al invite Bob to? ....

b What time is Bob going to meet Al? ....

c Where are they going to meet? ....

d How long does Al have for lunch? ....

e When did Al's lunch finish? ....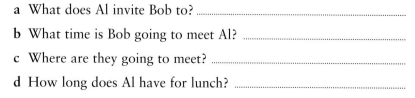

2 Listen to Bob on Track 37 again. Underline the words and syllables that he stresses most. The first one is done for you.

a <u>Hi</u>. Nice to <u>see</u> you.
b Yes, I'm fine. And you?
c Tonight? You've got tickets for the match tonight?
d And you're offering one of them to me?
e I don't know what to say.
f All right, then, yes please.
g I'll come round to yours if that's OK.
h That early?
i OK then. Do you think it's going to be cold?
j That sounds like pretty good advice.
k Oh right.
l Yes, I'll be there. Oh, and thanks a lot.

3 Listen to Track 38. This time you take Bob's part.

Example:

A: Hello.

YOU: Hi. Nice to see you.

A: Are you well?

YOU: Yes, I'm fine. And you?

Story reconstruction

1 Put the pictures in order to tell a story.

a

b

c

d

e

f

1 .... 2 .... 3 .... 4 .... 5 .... 6 ....

2 In your own words record the story onto a tape.

Listen to what you have recorded and make a note of any corrections you want to make.

Record your story again.

3 Listen to Martha telling the same story on Track 39.
How similar is it to yours?

AUDIOSCRIPT

Track 1

APRIL: You've got to be a really hard worker. Some jobs will come in on a Friday afternoon and they need to be done by Sunday morning, so you have to work over the weekend. ... umm ... you need to be able to work on your own as well as work with a team. You've got to be able to communicate with the others to understand if anything they're doing affects you ... umm ... you've got to be quite organised and quite decisive really.

Track 2

APRIL: I come from a very small village ... umm ... my father, well, he's half Irish. He's ... er ... a lorry driver, but he's always been really keen on engineering and he's always working on cars and bits and pieces. I suppose I picked up a bit from him and he's always been really interested in flying – he did a little bit himself – but then ... umm ... he got interested in the gliding club that moved to our village. I started going up in gliders with him to look around, you know, try it out, and then I got involved with that and learned to fly. Then that led me on to working for Marshall Aerospace.

INTERVIEWER: What sort of personal qualities do you think a good designer like you needs?

APRIL: You've got to be a really hard worker. Some jobs will come in on a Friday afternoon and they need to be done by Sunday morning, so you have to work over the weekend. ... umm ... You need to be able to work on your own as well as work with a team. You've got to be able to communicate with the others to understand if anything they're doing affects you ... umm ... you've got to be quite organised and quite decisive really.

You're doing a job that will affect an aeroplane and, even though about four other people check your work to make sure it's OK, it still comes down to you. You're responsible and you've got to make sure it's right.

INTERVIEWER: Most engineers are men, so what sort of qualities does a 22-year-old woman need working in a male environment?

APRIL: Yeah, umm. I think you've got to be able to prove yourself to people that might, might wonder how well you're going to do the job. ... umm ... You've got to show initiative really and ask questions and want to learn. You won't be very successful if you just sit there and just do the minimum. There'll always be I think that bit extra to do so that people will notice you for the right reasons, I suppose. But as a woman you are watched a lot. Well, not watched but people follow your progress more. When I worked on the planes in the hangars everyone knew me because I was the only girl there, so that now they all know my name and they all keep an eye on what I'm doing, how well I'm getting on – that's unusual. I know a lot of the male apprentices know very few people in the hangars even though they worked here for the same time, but when I worked in there a lot of people spoke to me to find out how I was getting on.

Track 3

WOMAN: Have you ever been in a life-threatening situation?

MAN: No, no, of course not. Oh, wait a minute, yes there was an incident once, well, it could have ended in tragedy. It was pretty frightening. It was when I was a kid, probably about six – five or six. We lived in the country. We had a big garden in those days.

WOMAN: That doesn't sound so terrible.

MAN: No ... but listen ... I was playing in the garden. I think it was in the summer. I was running around playing. And my mother had put these trunks out on the lawn.

WOMAN: Trunks?

MAN: Yeah you know, big suitcases. Old-fashioned things. She'd put them on the lawn to air them out. They were on their sides, open, so the sun and the air could get in.

WOMAN: I think I know what's coming.

Track 4

MAN: Yes, you probably do. So I came round the corner of the house and saw these trunks, and almost immediately got the idea that one of the trunks could be a boat, a pirate ship, that kind of thing. I thought it would be really exciting. So I put it flat on the ground and got in. I was the pirate captain. It felt great. Until the lid fell and shut tight.

WOMAN: What did you do?

MAN: I don't think I worried at first. I thought it would be easy to open it! Except that it didn't open. I couldn't get it open. I was trapped.

WOMAN: Oh no! You poor thing.

MAN: I tried everything. I pushed and screamed again and again. It was dark, very dark. I kicked with my feet. I called out for help, I remember.

WOMAN: Were you frightened?

MAN: What do you think? Of course I was. Pretty soon I was absolutely terrified, to be honest.

WOMAN: So what happened?

Track 5

MAN: Well, my mother was in the house. She was doing some housework or writing a letter, something like that, and she suddenly realised that she hadn't seen me or heard me for a bit and after a while she thought this was a bit odd. So she called my name, she said, but no answer, so she started looking around the house, thank heavens, and she looked out of one of the upstairs windows and she suddenly saw that one of the trunks was there on the grass, tight shut. It only took her a second to realise what had happened. She was absolutely horrified. She ran down the stairs and out into the garden and once she'd opened the lid she pulled me out, half-unconscious, seriously shocked, and frightened out of my wits!

WOMAN: I bet you were.

MAN: I certainly was. Do you know, I'd forgotten all about that until you asked me.

WOMAN: I'm surprised you're not claustrophobic.

Track 6

PETER: ... they will just have to start talking if they want the peace process to continue. And now back to you, Jim, in the studio in London.

JIM: Well, that was Peter Janus reporting from the United Nations. Now for our next piece we're going over to Sue Ballot in Vaness, north-west France with an incredible story of survival.

SUE: Yes Jim, and it is an incredible story. Yesterday, a married couple, Kevin McIlwee and his wife Beverly, both of them from the island of Jersey, had a miraculous escape after plunging 10,000 feet when their parachutes failed to open properly. They broke a number of bones, but amazingly they're still alive.

I should explain that Kevin (he's 47) and Beverly (just three years younger) were on their honeymoon. Mr McIlwee is a parachute instructor, and persuaded his new wife to do a tandem jump – that's when an instructor jumps with someone (in this case Beverly) strapped to him.

The accident happened when the first parachute didn't open properly. Mr McIlwee tried to solve the problem, but when he couldn't, he tried to get rid of that chute and use the second, emergency parachute that skydivers always carry with them.

A few hours ago I spoke to Beverly's father, Dennis Murtaugh, who explained what happened next. His words were spoken by an actor because the line was not good when we talked.

DENNIS: Unfortunately, Kevin wasn't able to jettison the first parachute properly so the emergency chute wouldn't open and they just fell faster and faster. Kevin told me that they thought that was it, they were going to die.

SUE: So how did they survive?

DENNIS: It was pure luck, I suppose. I mean they only had half a parachute to slow them down. They hit the ground at an absolutely fantastic speed. It could have killed them.

SUE: How does your daughter feel about parachuting now?

DENNIS: She's never going to do another jump!

SUE: I'm not surprised.

DENNIS: She's only just starting to realise how lucky she is. When I spoke to her she said she was looking out of the window from her hospital bed enjoying seeing the daylight and the birds.

SUE: Beverly McIlwee needs a number of operations and will be in a wheelchair for weeks. She has broken bones in her leg, ankle and both of her feet. Her husband has a broken leg. Jim?

JIM: Thanks very much for that report Sue. Well, that's a honeymoon those two people will never forget! And now it's time for sport, so over to Simon …

Track 7

1

VOICE 1: One hundred, two hundred, three hundred, four hundred …

VOICE 2: Numbers. Numbers. That's all we hear these days. What do they mean?

VOICE 3: Do you want a new mobile phone?

VOICE 2: That's just what I mean. Numbers. Numbers. I just don't understand them. Which phone shall I choose?

VOICE 3: Relax. Help is at hand. At Phone Mobile our experts will help you through all those numbers and give you the only ones you need to know about …

VOICE 1: One hundred, two hundred, three hundred, four hundred …

VOICE 3: Like the new Applephone 500.

VOICE 2: FIVE HUNDRED?

VOICE 3: Yes, you heard it. Five hundred FREE minutes when you sign up with Applephone, just one of the great deals we've got for you. And all you have to do is call in at any branch of Phone Mobile, and we'll make those numbers disappear.

VOICE 4: Phone Mobile. We're here to help you with all those numbers.

2

WOMAN: Announcing the great Furniture Fanfare super summer sale.

MAN: We've got everything you might want at prices you won't believe.

WOMAN: How about a beautiful three-piece suite for only £400 in white, lilac, green or wine red?

MAN: Or a beautiful dining room table – seats up to eight people. Only £350.

WOMAN: And when you're tired what could be better than a beautiful king-sized bed by Slumber, the best bed builders in the country. It's so comfortable you fall asleep the moment your head hits the pillow.

MAN: Furniture Fanfare. Everything you need for the perfect home. At affordable prices. Come and visit us at Junction 26 on the M44.

3

MAN: Kid yourself it's OK to do a bit more than the speed limit. Everyone does it.
Kid yourself, speeding is OK if you don't get caught.
Kid yourself, you'll never lose control. You're cool.
Well don't kid yourself. Driving too fast for the conditions causes one in three of all deaths.
So, how fast are you going now? What's the speed limit? Think about it. How would you feel if you killed a kid?

WOMAN: Think about it.
Good driving is no accident. It's right under your right foot. Don't kill a child. Kill your speed.

MAN: A message from the CCC road safety campaign.

4

WOMAN: Don't you just hate all that noise and fuss, standing in queues, and then when you get to talk to the assistant she doesn't know the answer to your question – that's if her computer is working. But that's what it's like when you go to most high-street travel agents to book your annual holiday.

MAN: Well, now you can avoid all that inconvenience and book your holidays direct from your home. All it takes is the click of a mouse.

WOMAN: Yes. Visit us at Getawaybreak.com and you can find exactly what you want right there.

MAN: Getawaybreak.com. The place everyone wants to visit. And you won't have to wait to be served!

Track 8

WOMAN: Excuse me, sir.

MAN: Yes. What?

WOMAN: Can you give me just a few minutes of your time?

MAN: It's not very convenient. I'm in a bit of a hurry.

WOMAN: It'll only take a second.

MAN: A second. I don't think so.

WOMAN: OK, then a couple of minutes.

MAN: Look, I'm really busy. I don't think …

WOMAN: Oh please, sir. If you answer just a few questions you'll automatically be entered into our prize draw.

MAN: Sorry?

WOMAN: Our prize draw. Everyone who takes part in this survey is entered into our prize draw, which takes place in three weeks.

MAN: What's the prize?

WOMAN: A holiday for two in Jamaica.

MAN: What are my chances of winning?

WOMAN: The same as anybody else's, I suppose.

MAN: How many people are taking part in this survey?

WOMAN: I wouldn't know.

MAN: Look, this is really …

WOMAN: Come on sir, you've spent a couple of minutes talking to me already. You might as well answer a few questions.

MAN: Oh all right, if you must. But let's get a move on.

WOMAN: Right, well the first question is 'How often do you go shopping? Once a week, twice a week, three times a week or more than three times a week?'

MAN: Oh, once a week – but only if I have to!

WOMAN: Yes … and how many items do you usually buy when you go shopping: one, two, between three and five, between six and ten or more than ten?

MAN: I don't know, really. I suppose, well, usually it's a couple of things. No more than two anyway.

WOMAN: I'll put two then. The next question is 'How much time do you spend when you go shopping, an hour …'

MAN: I don't understand the question.

WOMAN: Well, when you go shopping how long do you spend for the whole expedition? Less than an hour, between one and two hours or more than two hours?

MAN: Oh. less than an hour, if possible. I mean it's not something I do for fun!

WOMAN: OK, the fourth question, 'When you go shopping for clothes what do you buy most often, trousers, shirts, underwear, T-shirts, jackets or sweaters?'

MAN: I've absolutely no idea.

WOMAN: Well just say one of them, any one.

MAN: Any one?

WOMAN: Yes. Why not?

MAN: All right. Trousers.

WOMAN: Right. The last question, 'What is your favourite colour for a pair of trousers?'

MAN: Never thought about it.

WOMAN: Yes but if you did?

MAN: Black, I suppose.

WOMAN: Right, well that's it. Now if you'd just like to write your name and address here your name will go forward for the prize.

MAN: The holiday in Jamaica.

WOMAN: Yes! If you're lucky, you'll be flying to Jamaica.

MAN: I won't be. I never am.

WOMAN: Don't be so pessimistic. You never know.

MAN: Oh yes I do. I never win anything!

Track 9

TONY: Yes, well, we've got two young children so we have to choose our holidays with them in mind. That's why we come to places like this. Well, it's much more enjoyable than having bored children in some hotel in the middle of a big city. They can play with other children all day, go swimming or boating, that kind of thing. And you know camp sites are getting better and better. They've got excellent facilities these days. You should try it.

SANDRA: I like, you know, adventure holidays, backpacking, walking in the mountains, that kind of thing. I don't like tourist resorts. I prefer somewhere off the beaten track. But it's getting more and more difficult to find places like that. This year I've already been to Scotland, which was the most fantastic experience, and next month I'm going trekking in the foothills of the Andes in Peru. A friend of mine went pony-trekking in Iceland once. I'd like to try that.

JOSETTE: Oh, there's no doubt about it. We just love a bit of luxury and lazing around. That's why we go on cruises. We come back a bit fatter, of course, but we feel good too and we've been to places we don't normally go to. We need to be a bit richer than we are, though. Cruises seem to be the most expensive vacations in the world. But you do meet nice people, that's the best bit.

MEERA: Now that I'm getting older I'm not as energetic as I was. But I still love holidays with a bit of interest. I like a bit of culture, you see. So I generally visit galleries and museums or take sightseeing tours to monuments or other places of special interest. That's much more satisfying for me. Well, I am bored by tourist resorts – all that noise, everyone trying so hard to enjoy themselves. Maybe it's all right when you're 20! But I'm a bit past that myself. And I don't sunbathe, you see. The most satisfying holiday I've had recently was a visit to Greece. The Parthenon is one of the most beautiful sights I've ever seen.

STEVE: I don't really care where I go. I just look for the best package deal, fly to some resort and have a ball. I like to go clubbing, so the place must have some nightlife. The noisier the better. So I go to bed at the crack of dawn and get up about lunchtime. Then I just lie by the pool all day until it's time to start partying again. Well no, that's not quite true. I have tried water-skiing and I went surfing in Australia once. But mostly I just chill out. Look, I work really hard, you know. Holidays are my chance to unwind.

Track 10

1

This is the last call for flight BA two four oh nine to Bogotá. Would all the remaining passengers on this flight please proceed to gate number 35 as this plane is now boarding.

2

Here is a platform announcement. The 6.52 to Kings Lynn will now depart from platform 4 and not from platform 1. Kings Lynn, platform 4.

3

Good morning, ladies and gentlemen. We're now ready to board the aircraft, flight BA two four oh nine to Bogotá. Could all passengers in rows 20 to 39 please come to the desk with their boarding cards and passports. Thank you very much.

4

West Anglia regrets to announce the delay of the 12.35 to London King's Cross. This train is running approximately 15, one five, minutes late.

5

Good afternoon ladies and gentlemen. Sorry for the delay. A train has broken down in front of us so we can't proceed, but they've told me they're working on it so we shouldn't be here for too long.

6

We will shortly be landing at Manchester airport. The captain has switched on the seatbelt sign so will all passengers please return to your seats, fasten your seat belts, fold your trays into the back of the seat in front of you and place your seats in the upright position.

7

Welcome to Manchester airport. For your own safety please keep your seatbelts fastened until the plane reaches the terminal building and the captain has switched off the seatbelt sign.

Track 11

It's cold and it's empty,
The light is getting dim.
I'm sitting here without you,
I don't feel like staying in.

'Home is where the heart is',
That's what I've been told.
But there ain't no heart beside me,
So I guess I'll hit the road.

[Chorus]
I'm making myself homeless
To see what I can find.
I'm not a pessimist or an optimist,
I just need to have some time.

And the light is bright at the road's end,
As I drive along in my van.
I'll sing about a sense of freedom,
And I'll forget about you if I can.
And the road stretches out before me.
I can go wherever I choose.
I can do whatever I feel like
'Cos I ain't got nothing, nothing to lose.

It's cold in this car park,
The rain is falling down.
There's no one here except for me,
As I go from town to town.

I'm sitting here in my mobile world
Enjoying my small space,
But it's getting rather lonely –
All I do is see your face.

[Chorus]

For what use is travelling without you?
It just makes me homesick for what I had.
I travel all day and I travel all night
And it isn't even good or bad.
But the road leads onwards forever
And I can't think of slowing down,
Until, one day, in the evening light
I see your face in town.
And you'll come running towards me,
And my travelling days will be done,
And we'll go back home one fine morning,
And we'll have our new day in the sun.

Track 12

AGENT: Come on in and have a look around.
PAUL: Thanks.
AGENT OK, so this is the kitchen.
HILARY: It's a bit cramped, isn't it?
AGENT: Yes, but look at the view.
PAUL: Yes, Hilary, that is pretty fantastic.
HILARY: Yes, I suppose so.
AGENT: OK, if you've seen enough here, let's go through into the living room.
HILARY: It's very cold here. Is it always this cold?
AGENT: Well, the house has been empty for the last seven months. The last tenants moved out in a hurry.
PAUL: Why?
AGENT We don't know. They just said they didn't like it any more. They left just like that. As if they were running away.
HILARY: Perhaps it was because of the cold.
AGENT: Oh no. The owners have had central heating put in – it's not on at the moment. Look, here in the living room there's a big fireplace.
PAUL: Oh, this is great. So light, really spacious. Don't you think so Hilary?
HILARY: Yes, it's lovely. What's the upstairs like?
AGENT: Come and see.
AGENT: Here we are. Here's the main bedroom.
PAUL: Oh yes. That's amazing. Just imagine waking up to that view. Every morning. I love this old cupboard.
AGENT: And if you'd like to come along here, you can see the second bedroom.
PAUL: Hilary! This is perfect. Small, just the right size. I can put a table in here. Yes, I can write in this room.
AGENT: You're a writer?
PAUL: Yes, that's why we want a house out here in the country. I'm finishing a novel.
AGENT: Have you had anything published?
PAUL: Well no, not yet, actually. But it's only a matter of time.
AGENT: And what do you do, madam?
HILARY: Well, I'm an actor. But I'm having a few months' rest at the moment.
AGENT: Interesting. Have I seen you in anything?
HILARY: Probably not. Most of my work is in radio.
AGENT: OK, so this is the bathroom.
HILARY: It doesn't have any windows.
PAUL: Yes, but that doesn't matter, love. I mean this house is perfect. No television, no telephone. I'm really going to like it here.
AGENT: So, you've decided?
PAUL: Yes.
HILARY: Can't we talk about it first?
PAUL: Nothing to talk about. We'll take it. For six months.

Track 13

INSPECTOR WADE: Well, everybody, as you know, Joshua Logan was killed early this morning. He was hit on the head with a blunt instrument – we don't yet know what. So I need to know what you were all doing last night. We can start with you, Arthur Logan. You are Joshua Logan's nephew, I think.
ARTHUR LOGAN: Yes, I'm staying here for a few days.
INSPECTOR WADE: Can you tell us about your movements?
ARTHUR LOGAN: Of course. In the middle of the night I was woken by a sound downstairs – a cry, I think. I looked at my watch. It was about a quarter past two in the morning. I pulled on some clothes and went downstairs.
INSPECTOR WADE: And what did you find downstairs?
ARTHUR LOGAN: Nothing … at first. You see, just as I was going towards the study I was attacked from behind … hit on the back of the head by a man, I think it was, with dark glasses and a black cap. I don't know how long I was unconscious. When I woke up I went to the study and there was my poor uncle Joshua … you know … I can't bear to think about it.
JULIET LOGAN: Poor Arthur.
INSPECTOR WADE: Now then, Juliet Logan, you are the dead man's wife, I believe. This must be very difficult for you. What can you tell me about the events of this morning?
JULIET LOGAN: Well, Inspector, last night I couldn't sleep. I have a lot on my mind. So I read until about two in the morning.
INSPECTOR WADE: You and your husband haven't been getting on well, I think.
JULIET LOGAN: Yes, it's no secret. I wanted a divorce, but he wouldn't agree.
INSPECTOR WADE: Some people in your situation might think of killing their husband.
JULIET LOGAN: Perhaps, but I didn't do it. I turned my light off at about five past two and went to sleep. I was woken by Arthur with the terrible news.
CRAWFORD JARVIS: It's not true.
INSPECTOR WADE: I'm sorry.
CRAWFORD JARVIS: It's not true, Inspector. Juliet's light was still on at 20 past two. I saw it.
JULIET LOGAN: Well perhaps I just went to sleep with it on and …
INSPECTOR WADE: And you are, sir?
ARTHUR LOGAN: That's Crawford Jarvis. He's a friend of my uncle's but he's crazy about my aunt. He's been in love with my aunt for years.
INSPECTOR WADE: Is that true, Mr Jarvis?
CRAWFORD JARVIS: Yes, yes, I admit it.
JULIET LOGAN: Oh, Crawford.
INSPECTOR WADE: So what were you doing last night?
CRAWFORD JARVIS: Well, I couldn't sleep either. I went for a walk in the garden. That's how I know about Juliet's light. And, Inspector, I must tell you – I have a black cap, it is true, but I didn't kill Joshua Logan, honestly.

Track 14

CRAWFORD JARVIS: And, Inspector, I must tell you – I have a black cap, it is true, but I didn't kill Joshua Logan, honestly.
INSPECTOR WADE: I know you didn't, Mr Jarvis.
CRAWFORD JARVIS: Well then, who did?
INSPECTOR WADE: Arthur Logan, I arrest you for the murder of your uncle Joshua Logan. You do not have to say anything, but anything you do say may be taken down and used in evidence.
ARTHUR LOGAN: But … but … how did you know?
INSPECTOR WADE: How did I know? Because you're not very clever. That's how I knew. Attacked from behind, you said. Hit on the back of the head. Yet you said that you saw the man with a black cap and dark glasses! Even though he was behind you. Really! The most obvious lie in the world. Come on!

Track 15

JANE: So, do you like living here, Hilary?

HILARY: Yes. It's a great place to rent while Paul is writing his novel. But I wouldn't like to live here forever.

PAUL: It's got ghosts, apparently.

MARK: Oh don't be silly. Nobody believes in ghosts.

PAUL: Why not, Mark?

MARK: Paul! You're a rational human being. You can't believe all that stuff.

JANE: What's the story, then, about this place? Why does it have ghosts?

HILARY: Well apparently, Jane, about 300 years ago a family lived here. Mother, father, two kids. And one night …

PAUL: Terrible weather, wind, rain …

MARK: A night like this you mean?

HILARY: Yes, I suppose so, anyway there was a knock at the door, two men outside. They said 'Please can we stay the night.' They were cold and hungry. So they were given food and somewhere to sleep.

PAUL: But that night the whole family was murdered and the two strangers were never seen again.

HILARY: And that's why, on cold winter nights you can hear the family cry 'strangers, strangers' and sometimes they even …

JANE: What was that?

PAUL: Oh no! Not again. The electricity. I wonder how long we'll be without light this time.

MARK: Do you have any candles?

HILARY: Not sure. Have we got any left?

PAUL: I think so. I know where they are. I'll go.

HILARY: Thanks, Paul.

JANE: What was that?

HILARY: What was what?

JANE: That noise.

HILARY: I didn't hear a noise.

JANE: There. Listen.

MARK: Oh come on love, you're being silly.

JANE: I'm really cold. Anyone else cold?

HILARY: Yes. Suddenly … it's suddenly cold.

GHOSTLY VOICE: Strangers in the house … strangers in the house.

JANE: Did you hear that?

MARK: It's just Paul playing around. Paul? Paul?

JANE: Oh my God, what was that?

MARK: It's OK, leave this to me. I'll go and see.

HILARY: No Mark, stay here.

MARK: It's OK. Back in a minute.

JANE: I don't like this, Hilary.

HILARY: No, neither do I.

JANE: Paul? Mark? Paul? Mark?

HILARY: I hate being in the dark like this. Can't see anything … I … it's … Oh no …

JANE: Hilary. Hilary. Hilary. Hilary …

Track 16

CHARLIE: And now, at five past eight here on Breakfast Television, it's time for our weather report from Samantha Sweet. Good morning, Sam.

SAM: Hello Charlie, and good morning to all of you watching. As usual, everything depends on where you live this morning. Some of you will be luckier than others. We've got everything: rain, heavy snowfall, freezing conditions, but sunshine too. Right, so let's start with the south-west of the country. As you can see from the chart, it's started quite cold – about 3 degrees centigrade – but it'll warm up as the day goes on, reaching about eight degrees by the afternoon. It's going to be cloudy with sunny periods, I think, but it's going to be a cold night, though, down below freezing – about minus 1, I should think. So be warned!

In the south-east, things are much the same, though not quite as warm as in the south-west. But I don't expect temperatures to fall below freezing tonight. That's because of a warmer breeze coming in from the Channel.

In the middle of the country, things are a bit more confused. Right now it's about 5 degrees centigrade, cloudy, and with some light rain. But that situation is going to change as the day goes on, and by the end of the day it will probably be raining quite heavily and the rain will continue through the night, only easing up tomorrow morning. But don't expect much dry weather in the next few days.

Things aren't quite so bad in Wales and the west. Here the rain will gradually die away in the late afternoon, so people can expect quite a dry night, though tomorrow looks like being a day of scattered showers.

Up the east coast of the country, in the north, and further north into Scotland it's pretty cold already, as anyone there knows. It's about minus 2 degrees centigrade, with heavy cloud, but that should go up to about 1 degree during the morning. But the outlook doesn't look good. Expect some snow by midday, starting quite light, but gradually increasing so that by the evening it will be heavy, with blizzard-like conditions on the road, so do be careful. In fact the police have just issued advice to motorists not to travel at all unless their journey is absolutely necessary. Temperatures tonight will drop to about minus 6 degrees.

And what of tomorrow? As I said, in the middle of the country, it's going to be wet and cloudy, scattered showers with the occasional burst of heavier rainfall. In the north and east, people should settle in for a cold spell with more snowfall over the next few days. Not quite so bad in the south and west, though. Here there will be some sunshine – when it isn't raining, that is.

And that's the end of this morning's forecast. Charlie?

CHARLIE: Thanks, Sam. By the way, you won't be worried about the weather for the next few days, will you?

SAM: No, Charlie, I won't. I'm off on holiday to the sunny Caribbean this afternoon for ten days.

CHARLIE: Well have a nice time, Sam, we'll miss you. And now back to our main news story this morning. The prime minister has announced …

Track 17

TODD: Thank you. Thank you. If you like what we're doing please put money in the hat. That's why we're here. And now here's our next dance. Start the music Rosa.

ROSA: Sure.

POLICE OFFICER: You can't do that here.

TODD: Excuse me?

POLICE OFFICER: You heard.

ROSA: What are you talking about? We are just entertaining people.

TODD: Are you telling us we can't dance for people?

POLICE OFFICER: That's right. You can't dance on the sidewalk like this. Unless you have a permit.

TODD: Do we have a permit, Rosa?

ROSA: We might do.

POLICE OFFICER: Well, I'm sorry, ma'am, 'might' isn't good enough. No permit, no dancing. You have to get a permit to do this kind of thing.

ROSA: Oh, don't be so cruel. Everybody loves our dancing.

POLICE OFFICER: Where are you guys from, anyway?

TODD: From Texas. Dallas, Texas.

POLICE OFFICER: I thought so. So that's your truck over there. The one with the Texas plates.

TODD: Er … yes.

POLICE OFFICER: Well, it's parked illegally, so you'd better do something about it.

TODD: Oh, surely we don't need to move it right now? Can we do it when we've finished?

POLICE OFFICER: Now listen here ...

ROSA: Do you know how to dance the tango, Officer?

POLICE OFFICER: The tango? Me? Oh no!

ROSA: Come on! You should try it.

POLICE OFFICER: Well I don't know ...

ROSA: Come on, Todd. Put on the music.

POLICE OFFICER: Hey wait! Wait!

ROSA: Not bad, Officer. Not bad!

POLICE OFFICER: Hey, this is fun. Yeah, I could ... could really like this. I really could. Hey wait! Oh no!

SENIOR OFFICER: Officer Bradley! Officer Bradley! What on earth do you think you're doing?

POLICE OFFICER: Uh ... what ... er ... hello, sir.

SENIOR OFFICER: Bradley?

POLICE OFFICER: Yes sir?

SENIOR OFFICER: Back to the precinct now. Wait in my office. You've got some explaining to do.

Track 18

1

MAN: Excuse me. ... Excuse me.

YOUNG WOMAN: Sorry? What's the problem?

MAN: Could you turn that thing off?

YOUNG WOMAN: Sorry? What was that?

MAN: Listen, take your headphones off!

YOUNG WOMAN: Sorry?

MAN: Take your headphones off.

YOUNG WOMAN: All right, all right.

MAN: Listen, I can't stand your machine. Ticka ticka ticka all the time. It's driving me mad.

YOUNG WOMAN: All right, all right. I'll go and sit somewhere else.

MAN: Yes, why don't you do that.

YOUNG WOMAN: Cor! Crazy old fool.

2

MAN 1: Hey you!

CYCLIST: Sorry? What?

MAN 1: Stop! Stop!

CYCLIST: Why, what's the matter?

MAN 1: Can't you read the sign?

CYCLIST: What sign?

MAN 1: Look. It means you can't ride on the pavement.

CYCLIST: Oh. Oh well, I didn't see it.

MAN 1: Well you've seen it now, OK?

CYCLIST: Yeah, I suppose so.

3

POLICEWOMAN: Excuse me sir.

MAN: Yes? What's the problem Officer?

POLICEWOMAN: Have you just eaten some crisps?

MAN: Yes, why?

POLICEWOMAN: And drunk a cola?

MAN: Yes. But I don't see ...

POLICEWOMAN: And you left the packet and the can on the grass.

MAN: Did I ...? Oh.

POLICEWOMAN: Yes, and that sign? What does that sign mean?

MAN: It means you mustn't drop litter. I suppose.

POLICEWOMAN: That's correct, sir. So what are you going to do?

MAN: I think I'm going to pick the packet and the can up.

POLICEWOMAN: That's exactly what I think, sir. Now isn't that a coincidence!

4

MAN: And so I said to Martin, well, if you're going to be like that ... what ... Oh ... well ... I'm on the train ... yes, well Martin said that the foreign ...

WOMAN: I can't stand this. I really can't.

DAUGHTER: Oh Mum, leave it out.

WOMAN: No, I'm going to say something!

DAUGHTER: Why?

WOMAN: Because I don't want to have to listen to his conversation. It's driving me crazy!

MAN: ... well, of course, Martin was completely amazed because I was right, I mean, I don't want to boast or anything ...

WOMAN: Excuse me!

MAN: ... but I am cleverer than Martin.

WOMAN: Will you please be quiet. Just be quiet. I can't stand it any more.

MAN: Er ... what? ... Nothing, mate, nothing ... Listen ... got to go. Bye.

WOMAN: Well, thank you.

DAUGHTER: Oh Mum!

Track 19

POLICEMAN: Good morning, Madam.

WOMAN: Morning.

POLICEMAN: I hope you didn't have any trouble getting here.

WOMAN: No. My son brought me, thank you very much.

POLICEMAN: Oh, good.

WOMAN: So what do you want me to do?

POLICEMAN: Look through this window if you don't mind.

WOMAN: Ah yes. At the men.

POLICEMAN: That's right, Madam.

WOMAN: All right. I'm looking. What now?

POLICEMAN: Well, I want you to take your time. Study the men very carefully.

WOMAN Oh, no need.

POLICEMAN: Sorry?

WOMAN: There's no need.

POLICEMAN: What, you mean you can see the man who took your dog?

WOMAN: Oh yes.

POLICEMAN: Well, who is it?

WOMAN: That one.

POLICEMAN: Which one?

WOMAN: The one with the beard.

POLICEMAN: There are three men with beards.

WOMAN: Yes.

POLICEMAN: So which one is it? Please.

WOMAN: The man in a green jacket.

POLICEMAN: Yes, but there are two men with green ...

WOMAN: Look! That one.

POLICEMAN: Which one?

WOMAN: The one scratching his ear.

POLICEMAN: But he doesn't have a green jacket.

WOMAN: Doesn't he?

POLICEMAN: No. It's red.

WOMAN: Ah. Well that explains it.

POLICEMAN: It does?

WOMAN: Yes. My eyes aren't what they used to be, you see.

POLICEMAN: But can you still be sure that number five is the man you saw?

WOMAN: Oh yes.

POLICEMAN: Good.

WOMAN: At least, I think so. I can't be absolutely sure.

POLICEMAN: You think so! You can't be sure?

WOMAN: Yes, well you see, I only saw him from behind!

Track 20

Good evening. Here is the news read by me, Alan Piper. A French climber was saved from almost certain death when she and her climbing companion used her mobile phone to call for help. Françoise Pilenko broke her ankle shortly after reaching the summit of K2, one of the most difficult climbs in the Himalayas. They were unable to signal to their colleagues waiting for them below because of appalling weather conditions. But Mrs Pilenko had her mobile phone with her, and despite poor reception, was able to phone her husband, Maurice, back home in Paris, France. Once he had got over his surprise, Mr Pilenko alerted the rescue authorities, who got both climbers off the mountain by helicopter. He is flying to Nepal to join his wife in hospital.

Computer experts have warned that a new virus, which has appeared in the last two days is one of the most dangerous that has ever been invented. Called 'Money for jam', it fills computer screens, which it attacks with pound and dollar signs, sends itself to other computers via its new host's email, and then destroys all the information on the computer's hard disk. Police are doing their best to trace the source of this latest danger, and have arrested two students in San Juan, Puerto Rico. Asked what can be done, Bella Karsfield, head of the computer research department at the University of Washington said that people should not open emails unless they are sure who has sent them.

An American woman has been arrested by police in Tuscaloosa, Alabama after a young British man discovered his Internet girlfriend was not in her thirties, as he thought, but was 65. Matt Runyon, from Oxford, England, met the love of his life on the Internet last September. Over the next few months he and his girlfriend, Monica Greenlife, sent each other daily emails and eventually agreed to marry. Matt travelled to Tuscaloosa from his home in England to meet his fiancée, but was shocked when he discovered that she had lied about her age. Matt Runyon is not talking to the press about his ordeal.

An Internet company, Mountain View, has just announced that it's to cease business after losing $70 million in two months. Mountain View, which sold holiday homes through its web pages, is just the latest dotcom company to crash. Financial analysts expect more business failures over the next few months as the economic situation gets more difficult.

In sport, Spanish tennis player Claudia Gonzalez Torrano has reached the final of the US Open, and at home, Manchester United have clinched their place …

Track 21

TOM: What do you want to study at university?

MICHELLE: Science.

TOM: Science?!

MICHELLE: Yes. I'm going to do combined chemistry and physics. What's wrong with that?

TOM: Well, I don't know. It's … it's just that, well, science!

MICHELLE: Sorry?

TOM: Well, I mean half the world's problems are because of science.

MICHELLE: Come again?

TOM: No look, I'm serious, I mean what have scientists ever done for us?

MICHELLE: What, you mean apart from giving us cars.

TOM: Well yes, apart from giving us cars …

MICHELLE: And aeroplanes.

TOM: OK, cars and aeroplanes, I agree, but look what they're doing to the planet: all that contamination, all that pollution, and you can't get anywhere because you get stuck in traffic jams …

MICHELLE: And don't forget the computer.

TOM: All right, all right, I agree, science has given us the computer too, but that's not so special, is it? I mean there are people all over the world who can't get anywhere near a computer. Anyway, they always crash.

MICHELLE: Oh, you're just being ridiculous!

TOM: Look, I accept that science has given us cars and planes and the computer, all right. But apart from them, what have scientists ever really done for us?

MICHELLE: What about medicine?

TOM: What <u>about</u> medicine?

MICHELLE: Well, without science and scientists most children wouldn't survive for more than about five years, and if we did make it into adulthood we'd all be dead before we were 50.

TOM: Well, I …

MICHELLE: Just think of all the drugs that keep people alive, all of them discovered by scientists. Think of the aspirin you take for a headache, the antibiotics that cure infections, all of those things.

TOM: Well, if science is so wonderful, how come we still don't know how to cure the common cold?

MICHELLE: Look, just …

TOM: And as for antibiotics, people have taken so many antibiotics that they don't work any more. There are new illnesses that are drug-resistant.

MICHELLE: Well yes, but who will find out how to get round that problem?

TOM: I haven't the slightest idea.

MICHELLE: Scientists, of course. 'What have scientists ever done for us?' What a stupid question.

TOM: It's not.

MICHELLE: Anyway, what are you going to study?

TOM: Film studies.

MICHELLE: Film studies?!

TOM: Yes. Why not?

MICHELLE: Oh come on. You can't be serious. I mean what have film makers ever done for us?

TOM: What, apart from making us laugh?

MICHELLE: Well yes, apart from making us laugh …

TOM: And making us cry.

MICHELLE: Yes, yes, I agree, and making us cry. Big deal! What's special about that? Anyway apart from laughing and crying, what have film makers ever done for us?

Track 22

Conversation 1

MAN: What do you think of that?

WOMAN: It's absolutely wonderful!

MAN: Look at that girl in the background … the way the sunlight catches her hair …

WOMAN: Yes, it's lovely.

MAN: … and all the farm workers in the foreground. They're so realistic. It's just so full of life.

WOMAN: Yes, it's wonderful. Now let's talk about something else.

Conversation 2

WOMAN: Look at that. Isn't it fantastic!

MAN: Is it?

WOMAN: Don't you think so?

MAN: Not really. Not my kind of thing at all.

WOMAN: Oh come on. Look at that girl in the background.

MAN: What about her?

WOMAN: The sunlight on her hair. Magical.

MAN: So what. She doesn't look like a real person at all. And all these people in the foreground, they're supposed to be musicians, are they?

WOMAN: It's art, Paul.

MAN: Well, perhaps I just don't like art!

Conversation 3

TEENAGER 1: Wow!

TEENAGER 2: Yeah.

TEENAGER 1: I mean, was that frightening or what?

TEENAGER 2: You're right. It was frightening. Absolutely terrifying. I was, like, so scared.

TEENAGER 1: Me too. I could hardly watch most of the time.

TEENAGER 2: Shall we see it again?

TEENAGER 1: Yes, yes, let's. It was so good.

TEENAGER 2: Brilliant!

Conversation 4

MAN 1: Did you enjoy that?

MAN 2: Of course I did. I absolutely loved it.

MAN 1: You didn't think it was a bit, you know, silly?

MAN 2: Silly? No. It was really good fun. I couldn't stop laughing.

MAN 1: I know. You laugh really loudly, you know.

MAN 2: Do I?

MAN 1: Yes, you do.

MAN 2: Well you hardly laughed at all.

MAN 1: I didn't think it was that funny.

MAN 2: You just don't have a sense of humour!

MAN 1: Well, thanks.

Conversation 5

WOMAN 1: Well, did you enjoy that?

WOMAN 2: Yes, of course. But it was pretty frightening, wasn't it?

WOMAN 1: That was half the fun!

WOMAN 2: Right. You know what was amazing?

WOMAN 1: No, what?

WOMAN 2: Well, we hardly ever actually saw the lady herself, did we? In fact, I'm not even sure if we did. But it was still pretty scary!

WOMAN 1: Yes, it was quite alarming once or twice.

WOMAN 2: You know what I think.

WOMAN 1: No, what?

WOMAN 2: There's nothing better than a good piece of live theatre.

WOMAN 1: Yes, you're probably right.

Track 23

TV COMMENTATOR 1: What a fantastic game! The atmosphere is absolutely electric, and with the score at one all it looks like we'll have to go into extra time and then, well, who knows what may happen. That's the thing about extra time, you never ...

TV COMMENTATOR 2: Yes, but it's not over yet. Liverpool are really putting on the pressure ...

ANGELA: Could you answer the phone, love?

GEOFF: I can't. You get it. I'm watching the game. There's only a few minutes left.

ANGELA: Geoff, please. I'm cooking. My hands are all messy.

GEOFF: Oh, all right. I suppose so. Hello? Oh hello Mum ... watching the football. Arsenal against Liverpool ... What? ... Yes, it's nearly finished ... Have you? You've seen a new car you want to buy? ... Well, I'm sure you can get a different colour. Look Mum, can I ring you back? ... Yes, of course I want to speak to you ... no, no, please don't be upset ... I just want to watch the end of this game. You know how important it is ... yes, I promise. In about five minutes or so.

ANGELA: Who was that?

GEOFF: My mother.

ANGELA: What did she want?

GEOFF: Tell you later.

GEOFF: Oh no. Not again.

ANGELA: Geoff!

GEOFF: All right, all right. Hello ... Hello, Clive ... you're feeling unhappy, are you? ... Well, if she doesn't want to go out with you, I would stop ringing her. But look, can I ring you back? It's the Cup Final ... I know you're my brother ... Yes, yes, I do care about you. But I'll ring you back ... because I don't want to talk to you right now. Goodbye.

ANGELA: Geoff?

GEOFF: Yes, what?

ANGELA: Can you just come here and help me? I can't open this tin.

GEOFF: Not now, Angela.

ANGELA: Oh please. If I don't get this thing open, we won't have any dinner.

GEOFF: But there's only a couple of minutes left, and if Liverpool score again.

ANGELA: Geoff! Please.

GEOFF: Oh all right. If I must ... Show me the tin. Come on. I haven't got much time ...

TV COMMENTATOR 2: ... and it's a cross to Owen and he's through the defenders, there's only the goalkeeper and he's past him so surely ... yes, goal! Goal! What a fantastic goal! And the crowd are on their feet ...

GEOFF: What? What? Oh no! They've scored. They've scored and I didn't see it.

ANGELA: Who's scored?

GEOFF: Liverpool. It's two one. They've almost certainly won the game.

ANGELA: Well, that's good, isn't it?

GEOFF: Well, of course it is, but I didn't see it.

ANGELA: Well, you can watch the – what do they call it – replay, surely.

GEOFF: Yes, but it's not the same ... it's just not ... oh what's the point!

ANGELA: Come on, Geoff, it's only a football game!

Track 24

SUSAN: ... because you wonder what – you know I wondered, 'What on earth am I doing here?' I thought, 'I may as well go home now' ... umm ... but I thought, 'No, I'm here I may ... you know, I've, I've got this far I may as well just see it through another 15 minutes and I can be out of here then, you know, if it goes all horribly wrong I never have to see these people again.'

Track 25

SUSAN: Umm ... went into a room where you could practise and then the accompanist came in and had a quick run-through ... umm ... and so you're waiting in a little room and you can hear other people auditioning who sound ten times better than you, which then makes you even more frightened because you wonder what – you know I wondered, 'What on earth am I doing here?' I thought, 'I may as well go home now' ... umm ... but I thought, 'No, I'm here I may – you know, I've, I've got this far I may as well just see it through another 15 minutes and I can be out of here then, you know if it goes all horribly wrong I never have to see these people again.' ... umm ... So then went into a room where there was two people who were auditioning you and the accompanist and you sat down with the music and played the accompanist accompanied piece ... umm ... and, er ...

INTERVIEWER: How did that go?

SUSAN: Some mistakes. I was just ...

INTERVIEWER: Because I bet you can remember just about every minute of it.

SUSAN: Oh, it was horrible. I hated it. Absolutely dreadful. I, I made mistakes. And I think because I was nervous I made mistakes ... umm ... and I wasn't used to playing with an accompanist because I don't have anybody to just practise with at home ... umm ... and any little mistake you make you think they're gonna, they know that you've made a mistake, they're very good musicians, they are going to be thinking 'Oh, she's dreadful, what on earth is she doing?' and I sort of breathed a huge sigh of relief when I ground to a – the end and nearly nearly felt like crying – I don't know, out of relief or just nerves that you've got to the end, yeah, just absolutely ... er ... it's w – a horrible moment moment ... erm ... and then they gave a piece of sight-reading to do, which wasn't too bad, actually it was better than I'd – had thought, and then a scale, I played a scale – I was so relieved when I played it in tune ... which is always a bit of a bonus when playing a scale, and then, and then they said to me, they said, 'Oh ... umm ... will you be at orchestra on Monday?' because this was on a Saturday and I said, 'Well, kind of depended on today really', and they said, I said, 'When will I get to know?' and they said that the person who sorts out the auditions would phone me ... umm ...and so they said, 'Oh come along on Monday', so I thought, well, do I take that as a 'yes' or do I take that as … umm…? You know, you just don't know, so I went home and I was actually going out that evening and quickly phoned my parents and said, 'Er, dreadful! Horrible! They'll ring me', and nobody phoned me for the rest of the weekend. Monday evening ca – time to go to orchestra, nobody had phoned me so I thought, well I'd better go because nobody's told me not to go, and … umm … they – someone came up to me just before we started and – no, actually, I think it was in the interval – and said, 'Oh I'm pleased you got in', which after all that, 'n' you know to me it was such a big thing – you know, I'd been practising for a long time – when it's something that you want to do and just suddenly … err … you're in.

Track 26

WOMAN: Hi. What's your name?
MAN: What do you do?
WOMAN: Oh really? Do you like the job?
MAN: What's the best thing about it?
WOMAN: What's the worst thing about it?
MAN: What time do you get to work?
WOMAN: What time do you leave work?
MAN: What do you have for lunch every day?
WOMAN: What do you like doing at the weekend?
MAN: Thanks for talking to us. Bye.

Track 27

MARTHA: One evening Pete and Tabitha decided to go out for dinner. They left the house at 7.30 and drove to their favourite restaurant.
They had a lovely meal. When it was over they asked for the bill, but when the waiter brought it over they realised they had a problem. Tabitha hadn't brought her bag, and Pete couldn't find his wallet. Suddenly he remembered that he'd left it at home. He left Tabitha in the restaurant, got into the car and drove home. But when he got there he realised that he'd left his house keys inside the house, too! He didn't know what to do. He drove back to the restaurant and explained the situation to the manager. But the manager wasn't pleased. He wasn't pleased at all. And that's why Pete and Tabitha ended up washing dishes all night.

Track 28

MATTHEW: I think that tourism is a bad thing because it makes people fly all over the world and, according to many scientists, 15 per cent of all greenhouse gases will come from aeroplanes by 2050. And as more aeroplanes fly it gets more dangerous up there in the sky.
And that's not all. Tourism has a bad impact on the places where tourists go. Water is diverted from agricultural areas – and the poor suffer.
Tourism generates a lot of rubbish. It destroys countryside and wildlife disappears. And worst of all it destroys traditional customs.
Those are some of the reasons why I don't approve of tourism.
MARTHA: I am in favour of tourism because, more than anything else, it's fun. It benefits local economies and anyway, it's the world's largest industry.
One of the most important aspects of tourism is that it provides employment for many people who wouldn't have a job without it. And tourism helps the different peoples of the world understand each other.
If tourism is restricted, only the rich will be able to travel, and that would be a great pity. Everyone needs a chance to unwind, and that's what tourism provides.

Track 29

MATTHEW: OK, on your piece of paper draw a house. It's got two floors – that's two storeys. There's a big chimney for the smoke. It's quite an old house.

There's a garden at the front and at the sides. At one side of the house there's a garage for the car. There's a fence with a garden gate, too.
The front door is in the middle of the house and there are big windows on either side of the door. There are three windows on the first floor.
There are three people in the garden. A woman, a man and a child.
It's a beautiful day. The sun is shining, but there's a big black cloud in the sky so perhaps it's going to rain.

Track 30

MARTHA: Draw a picture of a tall house. It's got four floors – that's four storeys. Each storey has two windows. The front door to the house isn't actually at the front, it's at one side of the house. There are steps leading up to it. The house has got two tall chimneys.
In front of the house there's a car parked on the street.
It's pouring with rain – a terrible day. There's a really sad, wet dog on the pavement. It looks really miserable!

Track 31

MATTHEW: Hello, what's your name?
Nice to meet you. How are you?
Well anyway, what kind of a house do you live in?
Do you like where you live or would you like to change it?
I know this is a difficult question, but can you imagine yourself in ten years? What do you think your life will be like then?
What's your idea of perfect happiness?
What's your favourite food?
Who's the most important person in your life?
I hope we meet again sometime. Bye.

Track 32

Marianne's dream

When Marianne started a new picture she often had the same dream when she went to sleep. In the dream she went to Malapa, the biggest city on the mainland. She walked along the main street with her pictures under her arm. She went into a shop and sold them for a lot of money. Then, in her dream, she went to a department store and bought a wonderful dress, some pretty shoes and a beautiful coat.
After that, she went back to the first shop and looked at her pictures in the window. A lot of people were buying them. One man bought three. He was tall, he had dark hair and he was very good-looking.
'Who painted these pictures?' he asked the shop assistant.
'That girl there', came the answer.
The good-looking man walked up to Marianne. 'I've never seen paintings like these before,' he said. 'One day you'll be very famous. People will buy your pictures all over the world.'
Marianne was very happy. 'How do you know that?' she asked.
'Pictures are my business,' he answered. 'I buy and sell them. Will you come and have dinner with me? I want to talk about your paintings.'
They had dinner together. The man said, 'Your paintings are beautiful. But you are even lovelier than your paintings.'
They danced together that night and they fell in love. Soon they were married, and then they went round the world together.
Marianne painted hundreds of pictures. She was famous.
That was Marianne's dream.

Track 33

What's the weather like?
How many tables are there in the café?
Remember the girl playing the guitar. Can you describe her – what she's wearing, her hair, that kind of thing?
How many other girls are there at the table with the singer?
There's a man reading a newspaper. Can you remember what his wife is doing?

Can you describe the wife – Lucy, her name is?
Can you describe the man reading the newspaper?
At one table there's just one young man. Can you describe him?
What's he doing?
Did you see what the waiter had on his tray?
Does anyone in the picture have a pen in their mouth?
How many people in the picture have sunglasses?

Track 34

WOMAN: What's the weather like?
MAN: Fantastic! Hot and sunny.
WOMAN: How many tables are there in the café?
MAN: There are three – in the picture anyway.
WOMAN: Remember the girl playing the guitar. Can you describe her – what she's wearing, her hair, that kind of thing?
MAN: Well, she's got long blonde hair. She's wearing a pink T-shirt and shorts – cut-off jeans, actually.
WOMAN: How many other girls are there at the table with the singer?
MAN: Three.
WOMAN: There's a man reading a newspaper. Can you remember what his wife is doing?
MAN: Yes. She's talking to someone on her mobile phone.
WOMAN: Can you describe the wife – Lucy, her name is?
MAN: OK. She's got white hair. She's wearing a straw hat and a blue dress. She's got sunglasses on.
WOMAN: Can you describe the man reading the newspaper?
MAN: Yes. He's about 50, 55. He's got a beard. He's quite fat. He's wearing a blue shirt and red shorts.
WOMAN: At one table there's just one young man. Can you describe him? What's he doing?
MAN: He's got long dark hair. He's wearing a white T-shirt and blue shorts. He's leaning back with his arms folded and his legs crossed.
WOMAN: Did you see what the waiter had on his tray?
MAN: There was just a cup of coffee or something, wasn't there?
WOMAN: Does anyone in the picture have a pen in their mouth?
MAN: Yes. The young man, Andy, does.
WOMAN: How many people in the picture have sunglasses?
MAN: Two. Lucy and Andy.

Tracks 35 and 36
A
ANNE: Hello, John. What's the matter?
JOHN: I can't get this printer to work.
ANNE: Have you switched it on?
JOHN: Yes, of course I have.
ANNE: Are you sure?
JOHN: Of course I'm sure.
ANNE: OK.
JOHN: At least I think I'm sure.

B
MARIA: Hello. Hello. Can you hear me?
CHARLES: Yes, I can hear you fine. Where are you?
MARIA: I'm on the train.
CHARLES: On the train? What time will you be home?
MARIA: In about an hour.
CHARLES: An hour? But you said …
MARIA: Yes, I know. I'm late. Sorry.

Track 37
AL: Hello.
BOB: Hi. Nice to see you.
AL: Are you well?
BOB: Yes, I'm fine. And you?
AL: Yes, I'm fine too, thanks. Hey, I've got two tickets for the match tonight. D'you want to come?

BOB: Tonight? You've got tickets for the match tonight?
AL: That's what I said.
BOB: And you're offering one of them to me?
AL: Yes, that's the general idea.
BOB: I don't know what to say.
AL: Well, yes or no would be a possibility!
BOB: All right, then, yes please.
AL: Fantastic. Shall I come round to your place or will you come to mine?
BOB: I'll come round to yours if that's OK.
AL: Yes, that's fine. Can you be there by about 6.30?
BOB: That early?
AL: Yes. If we're to get to the match on time.
BOB: OK then. Do you think it's going to be cold?
AL: Dunno. I haven't heard the forecast. But I'd dress up warm if I was you.
BOB: That sounds like pretty good advice.
AL: Look, I've got to go. My lunch hour finished five minutes ago.
BOB: Oh right.
AL: So see you at 6.30?
BOB: Yes, I'll be there. Oh, and thanks a lot.
AL: Don't mention it. Bye.
BOB: Bye.

Track 38
AL: Hello.
[Pause]
AL: Are you well?
[Pause]
AL: Yes, I'm fine too, thanks. Hey, I've got two tickets for the match tonight. D'you want to come?
[Pause]
AL: That's what I said.
[Pause]
AL: Yes, that's the general idea.
[Pause]
AL: Well, yes or no would be a possibility!
[Pause]
AL: Fantastic. Shall I come round to your place or will you come to mine?
[Pause]
AL: Yes, that's fine. Can you be there by about 6.30?
[Pause]
AL: Yes. If we're to get to the match on time.
[Pause]
AL: Dunno. I haven't heard the forecast. But I'd dress up warm if I was you.
[Pause]
AL: Look, I've got to go. My lunch hour finished five minutes ago.
[Pause]
AL: So see you at 6.30?
[Pause]
AL: Don't mention it. Bye.
[Pause]

Track 39
One day Michael saw Catherine sitting alone in a café. He thought she was beautiful so he went over to her and started talking to her. He rang her the next day and asked her out. Pretty soon they were boyfriend and girlfriend. But one day Catherine was walking in a park when she saw Michael with another girl. She was very angry and asked him what he was doing. The other girl soon became angry as well and they both told him to go and jump in the lake! Now Michael just sits on his own every evening watching the sun go down and feeling miserable.

ANSWER KEY

PART A: LISTENING

LISTENING 1

1
design engineer

2
a Her father did.
b She thinks it's a good thing (you get noticed, people know who you are), although there is a lot of pressure to prove yourself.

3
a F (He's half-Irish.)
b T
c T
d T
e T
f T
g F (She used to work in the hangars.)
h F
i F

4
a ✗
b ✓
c ✓
d ✓
e ✓
f ✗
g ✗
h ✗
i ✗
j ✗
k ✗
l ✗
m ✗
n ✗
o ✓
p ✓

5
a He's always liked it a lot.
b small little parts of engines and things like that
c a small amount
d started to do a lot of it (and liked it)
e it's your responsibility
f do the smallest amount of work that you can do
g look at/watch
h how things were going/how I was managing in the job

LISTENING 2

1
a the water tank
b the ladder
c the lawnmower
d the garden shed

2
a (1) 5 or 6 years old
   (2) She had put some trunks on the lawn because she wanted to air them out.
b (1) Because he pretended it was a boat (and he was a pirate).
   (2) The lid fell and shut tight. The narrator kicked and screamed. He called out for help.
c (1) She realised that she hadn't seen or heard the narrator for some time.
   (2) She saw that one of the trunks on the lawn was tight shut.
   (3) She ran into the garden, opened the trunk and pulled the narrator out. The narrator was shocked and frightened.

3
a a sailor who attacks ships and steals their contents
b unable to escape or get out
c anything above the ground floor in a house
d without being able to think (like being asleep)
e very frightened
f feeling nervous or scared because you are in a small, enclosed space

4
a pretty frightening
b would be really exciting
c I was absolutely terrified
d was absolutely horrified
e seriously shocked

LISTENING 3
a F
b T
c F
d T
e F
f T
g F

2
a Kevin and Beverly
b Sue
c Jim
d Beverly (and probably Kevin)
e Peter
f Kevin and Beverly
g Dennis
h Beverly
i Kevin
j Beverly

3
a first parachute
b solve the problem
c emergency chute
d first parachute
e emergency chute
f faster and faster
g going to die
h pure luck
i hit the ground

LISTENING 4

1
Commercial 3 is the odd one out because it is not selling a product or a service. It is asking people to drive more slowly.

2
a 3
b 4
c 1
d 2

3
a 500 free minutes
b all those numbers
c £400 for a sofa and two chairs (three-piece suite)
d £350 for a beautiful dining room table
e one in three of all deaths
f yourself
g your speed
h all that noise and fuss
i www.getawaybreak.com

5
a at hand
b great deals
c Call in
d super summer sale
e you might want ... you won't believe
f All it takes
g wants to visit

LISTENING 5

1 once a week
2 two items
3 0–59 minutes
4 trousers
5 black

2

a I'm in a bit of a hurry. [7]
b You'll automatically be entered in our prize draw. [5]
c What are my chances of winning? [6]
d I wouldn't know. [2]
e But let's get a move on. [4]
f But only if I have to. [8]
g It's not something I do for fun. [3]
h Don't be so pessimistic. You never know. [1]

LISTENING 6

2

a Steve
b Meera
c Sandra
d Josette
e Tony

3

a Sandra
b Steve
c Josette
d Tony
e Meera
f Sandra
g Steve
h Sandra
i Meera

LISTENING 7

2

a 5
b 2
c 4
d 1
e 7
f 3
g 6

3

a last call [d]
b proceed [d]
c announcement [b]
d board [f]
e regret ... delay [c]
f running ... late [c]
g Sorry [a]
h shouldn't [a]
i return [g]
j Fasten [g]
k Place ... position [g]
l fastened ... switched off [e]

LISTENING 8

2

a a feeling that you are free
b a van that you can sleep in
c to go travelling
d anywhere that you feel comfortable is your home
e to not have a home
f to feel as if you do not have any friends
g someone who thinks everything will be wonderful
h someone who thinks everything will be terrible

3

First verse
The correct order is **c, d, b, a.**
Last verse
The correct order is **h, e, g, f.**

4
The best summary is **b.**

5

a hit the road
b pessimist ... optimist
c some time
d bright ... end
e I can
f out before me
g I feel like
h without you
i what I had
j forever

LISTENING 9

1

a 5
b 2
c 4
d 3
e 1

2

a the second bedroom
b the kitchen
c the living room (it has a fireplace)
d the living room
e the main bedroom
f the second bedroom
g the bathroom

4

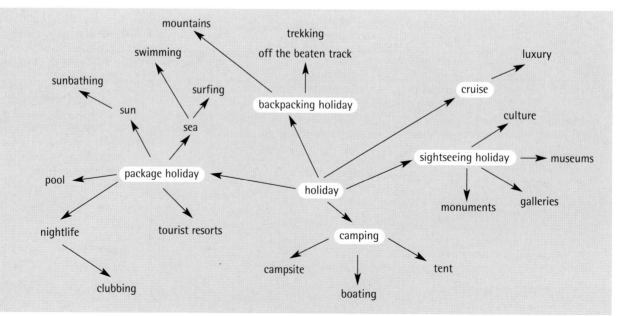

3
a Seven months.
b They just said they didn't like it any more.
c He's writing a novel.
d She's an actor.
e She's having a few months' rest.
f They take it. Paul decides.

LISTENING 10

1
a Joshua Logan's nephew.
b Arthur Logan's uncle and Juliet Logan's husband.
c Joshua Logan's wife (and widow).
d A friend of Joshua Logan's. He is in love with Juliet Logan.

2
a Joshua Logan
b Arthur Logan
c Crawford Jarvis
d Crawford Jarvis

3
a Arthur Logan
b Arthur Logan
c Crawford Jarvis
d Juliet Logan
e Arthur Logan
f Juliet Logan
g Crawford Jarvis
h Inspector Wade
i Inspector Wade

5
She knew who killed Joshua Logan because Arthur said he saw the person who hit him from behind. You can't see someone behind you. He must have lied.

LISTENING 11

1
a 3
b 6
c 5
d 4
e 2
f 1

2
a T
b F
c T
d T
e F
f T
g P
h P
i F
j P

3
a living
b place
c writing
d forever
e don't
f ghosts
g human
h about
i again
j without
k any
l any
m think
n know
o I'll
p that
q what
r noise

4
a Anyone else cold?
b … it's suddenly cold.
c Strangers in the house…strangers in the house.
d you hear that?
e Paul playing around. Paul? Paul?

LISTENING 12

1

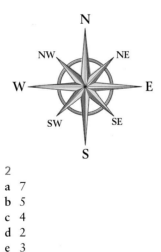

2
a 7
b 5
c 4
d 2
e 3
f 6
g 1

3
a 8.05am
b the south-west
c the north and Scotland
d to the Caribbean for a holiday

4

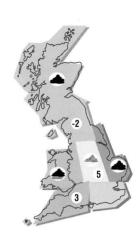

a Now

b Later today

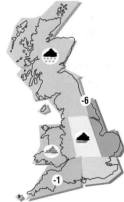

c Tonight

d Tomorrow

LISTENING 13

1

1 d
2 b
3 a
4 c

3

a pavement
b a document that gives you permission to do something
c licence plates (the letters and numbers at the front and back of a car)
d the police station of a certain area
e Madam (a polite form of address for a female – quite old-fashioned)

4

a can't do that [PO]
b can't dance [MD]
c might [FD]
d good enough [PO]
e have to get [PO]
f do something [PO]
g how to dance [FD]
h should try [FD]

LISTENING 14

1

a 2
b 3
c 4
d 1

2

a the sign [b]
b that thing off [d]
c eaten some crisps [b]
d stand this ... really [c]
e ride on the pavement [a]
f mustn't drop litter [b]
g me crazy [c]
h does that sign [b]
i be quiet [c]

3

a the man in picture a
b the woman in picture c
c the man in picture d
d the girl in picture c
e the police officer in picture b
f the man in picture c
g the young man in picture b
h the girl in picture d

LISTENING 15

2

She chooses man number 5.

3

a Her son brought her.
b Her dog.
c She says her eyes aren't what they used to be.
d Because she only saw him from behind.

4

a Morning.
b you didn't have any trouble getting here.
c My son brought me, thank you very much.
d Oh, good.
e what do you want me to do?

5

The word is *one*.

6

Example answer
He is short and quite fat. He is wearing a green jacket and black trousers. He has long, black hair and a beard.

LISTENING 16

1

a company collapse [✓] [4]
b computer virus [✓] [2]
c cure for cancer discovered [ ] [ ]
d earthquake [ ] [ ]
e election results [ ] [ ]
f Internet romance [✓] [3]
g mountain rescue [✓] [1]
h peace talks [ ] [ ]
i plane crash [ ] [ ]
j rocket launch for Pluto expedition [ ] [ ]

2

a A climber called her husband from a mobile phone when she was on a mountain.
b The climber was on K2. Her husband was in Paris.
c Police have arrested two students in Puerto Rico who, they think, created a computer virus.
d Bella Karsfield has warned people against the computer virus 'Money for jam'.
e The Internet romance was between someone from Oxford (UK) and someone from Tuscaloosa (USA).
f The man in the romance was 35, the woman was 65.

g The company, which lost $70 million, sold holiday homes on the Internet.

3

a Francoise Pilenko
b On the mountain K2
c Mr Pilenko
d Police are trying to trace the source of the computer virus 'Money for jam'.
e Matt Runyon and Monica Greenlife
f Monica Greenlife
g The Internet company Mountain View
h Financial analysts

LISTENING 17

1

a aeroplanes [✓]
b antibiotics [✓]
c aspirin [✓]
d biology [ ]
e cars [✓]
f chemistry [✓]
g computer [✓]
h cry [✓]
i injection [ ]
j laugh [✓]
k medicine [✓]
l physics [✓]
m ships [ ]
n shout [ ]
o space station [ ]
p university [✓]
q whisper [ ]

2

a Tom
b Michelle
c Michelle
d Michelle
e Michelle ... Tom ... Tom
f Michelle ... Tom
g Michelle ... Tom
h Tom
i Tom
j Tom ... Michelle
k Tom

3

a 1 contamination
  2 pollution
  3 traffic jams
b 1 Many people haven't got computers.
  2 Computers crash.
c 1 We can't cure the common cold.
  2 Antibiotics don't work with some infections.

4

a medicine
b scientists
c about
d make
e fifty
f drugs
g discovered
h headache
i infections
j wonderful
k common
l cold
m antibiotics
n antibiotics
o work
p illnesses
q find
r problem
s slightest
t Scientists

LISTENING 18

1

a conversation 5
b conversation 3
c conversation 2
d conversation 1
e conversation 4

2

a conversation 4
b conversation 1
c conversation 5
d conversation 4
e conversation 2
f conversation 3
g conversation 2
h conversation 1
i conversation 3

3

a in the background ... catches
b of life
c a real person ... in the foreground
d don't like art
e hardly watch
f couldn't stop
g pretty frightening
h nothing better than

LISTENING 19

1

a Geoff
b Angela
c Geoff
d Geoff
e Geoff's mother
f Clive (Geoff's brother)
g She can't open a tin
h A goal

2

a T
b T
c F (Liverpool 2, Arsenal 1)
d F
e F
f T
g F
h T
i F

3

Example answers
Conversation 1

a What are you doing?
b Has the game finished?
c Is the game nearly finished?
d I've seen a new car that I want to buy.
e The only problem is that it is red.
f Don't you want to speak to me?
g I'm really upset.
h Will you promise to ring me as soon as the game is finished?

Conversation 2

a Hello, Geoff. It's Clive.
b I'm feeling really unhappy.
c Yes, I keep ringing my girlfriend but she doesn't want to go out with me.
d Look, I am your brother.
e Don't you care about me?
f Why are you being like this?

LISTENING 20

1

Example answers

a play a prepared piece of music, play some scales (eight notes going up, eight notes going down), do some sight-reading (being given a piece of music you don't know and playing it straight away)
b act a prepared speech, read an extract from a play
c answer questions, wear decent clothes, ask questions
d play some of a game, train with the team, take a fitness test
e describe a picture, answer questions, talk to other students

2

The speaker is the nurse, Susan Bakewell.

3

a A music audition.
b Yes, she was successful.
c She hated it.

4

a usually a pianist who plays along with the solo player
b when the notes sound right, rather than ugly, because they are not too high or too low
c a quick rehearsal of a piece of music
d a series of notes going up and down with fixed intervals between them
e playing the music straight away, the first time you see it

5

a In the audition she had to play a piece of music with an accompanist, sight-read a piece of music, and play a scale.
b There were four people in the audition room (Susan, the accompanist and the two people auditioning).
c Saturday.
d Monday.
e She spoke to her parents about it.
f At the rehearsal on Monday.

6

a a huge sigh of relief
b see it through
c I can be out of here.
d I may as well ...
e Do I take that as ...?
f What on earth ...?

PART B: SPEAKING

SPEAKING 2

1

Picture A

a Two.

b No, they don't.

c The restaurant manager, a waiter and two cooks.

d They look very cross!

Picture B

e He's waiting for the customer (Pete) to pay the bill.

f He looks very frightened.

g (He is remembering) that he left his wallet at home.

Picture C

h They're in a restaurant.

i They look happy.

Picture D

j He's at his house.

k (He has gone there) to get his wallet.

l The house keys on the table.

Picture E

m The restaurant manager.

n (He is trying to explain) that his wallet is at home so he doesn't have any money.

o He is not at all happy.

p He's telling them to go and do the washing up.

2

1 C

2 B

3 D

4 E

5 A

SPEAKING 4

1

chimney **e**

fence **a**

garage **c**

gate **b**

window **d**

SPEAKING 6

1

a Marianne

b A tall man with dark hair

c Marianne

d Marianne and the tall dark man

e Marianne and the tall dark man

f Marianne

g When she starts painting a new picture

SPEAKING 9

1

a A (football?) match.

b At 6.30.

c At Al's house.

d 60 minutes.

e 5 minutes ago.

2

a <u>Hi</u>. Nice to <u>see</u> you.

b Yes, I'm <u>fine</u>. And <u>you</u>?

c To<u>night</u>? You've got tickets for the match to<u>night</u>?

d And you're offering one of them to <u>me</u>?

e I don't know what to <u>say</u>.

f All right, then, <u>yes</u> please.

g I'll come round to <u>yours</u> if that's OK.

h That <u>early</u>?

i <u>OK</u> then. Do you think it's going to be <u>cold</u>?

j That sounds like pretty good ad<u>vice</u>.

k Oh <u>right</u>.

l Yes, I'll <u>be</u> there. Oh, and <u>thanks</u> a lot.

SPEAKING 10

1

1 e

2 d

3 c

4 a

5 b

6 f